£3.50

Fast Castle: A History from 1602

FAST CASTLE
A HISTORY FROM 1602

Keith L. Mitchell   FSAScot

EDINBURGH ARCHAEOLOGICAL FIELD SOCIETY

ISBN   0 9513156 0 9

Printed in Scotland by J. Shepherd & Son Ltd.,

104 St. Stephen Street, Edinburgh, EH3 5AQ.

For my wife Helen

and

our children Diane and David

Acknowledgements

In the first instance I would like to acknowledge the particular debt of gratitude owed by the Edinburgh Archaeological Field Society to Mr. Frank Usher of Dunglass estate, and Mr. Tom Dykes of Redheugh Farm, without whose inspiration and support the Society would not have been formed. Their initial interest in our archaeological activities led us to carry out a thorough historical study of Fast Castle. Mr. Dykes has also been quick to respond to our questions concerning Dowlaw, and his knowledge of the farm and its immediate surroundings has been most useful.

My thanks also go to the staffs of the National Library of Scotland, Edinburgh City Libraries, the Royal Commission on the Ancient and Historical Monuments of Scotland, the University of Edinburgh, the Royal Museum of Scotland (formerly the National Museum of Antiquities), the Berwickshire District Library at Duns, and the Scottish Record Office, for their valuable assistance. The Keeper of the Scottish Record Office and Mr. Michael Bott, the Keeper of Archives and Manuscripts, University of Reading, kindly gave permission for extracts to be published from the Hall of Dunglass Muniments. I am grateful to Mr. George Bisset of Crathie, and Mr. J. A. Edwards, formerly Reading University Archivist, who made possible the transfer in 1976 of a large collection of Dunglass estate papers from that university to the Scottish Record Office.

Over a period of several years many members of our Society have helped with collecting information from libraries, mainly within Edinburgh. All these volunteers cannot be named, but three, Jennifer Dunbar, the late Mr. E. Gardiner (Gee), and Helen Mitchell, must receive special credit for their efforts. The translation of Latin documents, and in many cases the comprehension of archaic legal terminology, has posed recurring problems for our understanding of specific historical events. Thanks to the efforts of Dr. David Caldwell, Dorothy Ellen, Helen Aitken, and the late Mr. Dan Robertson, these difficulties have been largely overcome. Dr. Peter Anderson of the Scottish Record Office lent a sympathetic ear on points of interpretation relating to the lordship and barony of Coldingham, making several helpful suggestions. Between 1983 and 1985 a research team undertook the task of indexing, categorising, and generally interpreting the information used in this publication. The group included Maurice Carmichael, Eleanor Conolly, Val Dean, and Donald Whitehead, with some assistance from a few others. Prior to publication, several members of the Society undertook a variety of tasks which enabled the text and illustrations to reach the final stage far more quickly than would otherwise have been possible. Most notably, Val Dean spent many long hours typing and re-typing the drafts onto computer disks. Denis Smith, Hugh Robertson, and others, suggested initial corrections to the draft, while June Davidson, Jill Strobridge, and John Ward, assisted in obtaining information on some of the illustrations used. The text was edited by John Ward, and the proof copy checked by Mary Kennaway.

The publication of this history was financed by a most generous gift from an anonymous donor, to whom both I and the Society as a whole are very grateful. Thanks are due also to Thomas Tait and Sons, Ltd. of Inverurie, for donating paper used in preparing this publication, to Len Cumming for photographing many of the illustrations, and to all those, individually acknowledged, who have allowed maps and pictures in their custody to be reproduced.

Contents

List of Illustrations

Whoever reads this book will find
A thundering lot of lies are told,
But some perhaps may be inclined
To read and have the truth unfold.

[Found inscribed in a copy of Alexander A. Carr,
A History of Coldingham Priory (Edinburgh, 1836)]

Facing page: PLATE 1. Aerial view of Fast Castle, 1979.

PLATE 2. John Napier of Merchiston, 1550-1617.

1616

MATH. 1616.

ÆTATIS 66.

Introduction

In July 1594 a contract was signed at Edinburgh, between Robert Logan of Restalrig and John Napier of Merchiston, the celebrated inventor of logarithms [Plate 2]. Eighteen years earlier Logan had inherited Fast Castle, a stronghold built on a 100-150 feet high promontory running out from the Berwickshire sea cliffs, twelve miles to the east of Dunbar [Plate 1]. His contract with Napier records that 'as ther is dywarse reportis and appirancis that thair suld be within the said Robertes dwellinge place of fascastell a soum of monie and poise heid and hurdit vp secritlie quhilk as yit is on fund be ony man. The said Johne sall do his vtter and exact diligens to serche and sik out and be al craft and ingyne that he dow to tempt trye and find out the sam and be the grace of god ather sall find the sam or mak it suir that na sik thing hes been thair.' It also stipulated that when the conditions had been fulfilled, the contract was to be destroyed.[1] The terms of the agreement give a feeling of mystery and suspense, and little imagination is needed to visualise the two men planning their proposed treasure hunt. William Douglas, in his 1921 article on Fast Castle,[2] stated that the original manuscript was then held by Professor Glaisher of Trinity College, Cambridge, and that its survival raised doubts as to whether the search for treasure had ever taken place.[3] The contract's somewhat enigmatic details were resurrected from obscurity in 1969 when Fred Douglas, a retired Edinburgh bookseller, led an attempt to discover if any treasure might still remain hidden somewhere within the castle ruins. In conjunction with this treasure hunt, Douglas undertook historical research on various aspects of treasures he connected with the castle, leading to the publication in 1971 of his book *Gold at Wolf's Crag*.[4]

At about the same time, a few of those who had been associated with the treasure hunt formed themselves into an amateur archaeological association, with the initial aim of excavating specific areas of interest at Fast Castle. The association, which later became the Edinburgh Archaeological Field Society, decided in 1973 to begin a serious historical study of the castle, as a complement to the detailed information being produced by the excavations. At first it seemed that a lack of experience in historical research techniques threatened the venture's success. Persistence, however, brought to light several interesting publications, including William Douglas's essay. Although this work is reasonably comprehensive and impartial, with a copious bibliography, there are many omissions in its treatment of the period after 1602. However, the value of Douglas's article to our project cannot be overstated, and it remains a most informative history of the castle. Further investigation produced essential facts which filled many of the gaps in Douglas's account, particularly for the years between 1602 and 1687. Two of the most useful sources of information about Fast Castle's history during the seventeenth century are Thomson's *Coldingham Parish and Priory*,[5] and the article on Easter and Wester Lumsden published in the *History of the Berwickshire Naturalists' Club*.[6]

Some use has been made of manuscript material. In particular, records of the Dunglass estate, which over a considerable period included Fast Castle, contain a wealth of detail on the lifestyle of local tenant farmers and their workforce in the eighteenth and early nineteenth centuries. Dowlaw Farm has long been connected with Fast Castle and it is frequently mentioned in these papers.[7] From the various accounts ledgers and associated documents of Dowlaw, which span the period from 1741 to 1878, we have been able to obtain a much better understanding of how the land was used and what life was like for the ordinary people.

The Society has endeavoured to collect as much information on Fast Castle as time and circumstances permitted. The resulting accumulation of documentary evidence has unfortunately made it impossible to publish a complete account of the castle in one volume. In due course it is hoped to produce three further articles, covering the castle's early history to 1602.

Fast Castle before 1602

Due to the almost complete lack of documentation, Fast Castle's origins must remain obscure, and matters are complicated by the existence during the later middle ages of two castles with this name in the eastern Borders. The earliest reference to a Fast Castle found so far relates to the capture of a stronghold in 1333 by the Norfolk knight Sir Robert Benhale, after the Scots' defeat at Halidon Hill near Berwick. Exhaustive research, however, suggests that the description of this event, if true, relates to a castle in Roxburghshire near Jedburgh.[8] It is reasonable to assume that the Berwickshire fortress was standing in the fourteenth century, but no information has been discovered which sheds any light on its history during the period. Fast Castle begins to emerge from its cloud of dark mystery in a few official records by the first decade of the fifteenth century. During much of this time it seems to have been under English control. For example, in 1404 its commander, William Clifford, was ordered by Henry IV to give up 'fascastell' to the king's young son, John of Lancaster, Governor of Berwick, Warden of the Eastern Marches, and later Duke of Bedford. It is difficult to gauge the castle's contemporary strategic importance, although the defensive capabilities of its promontory site were probably more valuable at this time than later.

By what appears to have been a surprise attack, the castle was retaken for the Scots one night just before daybreak in 1410 when Patrick Dunbar, a son of the Earl of Dunbar, captured Thomas Holden, the English captain. A few years later William Haliburton was in occupation of either the Berwickshire or the Roxburghshire Fast Castle, and in 1419 he captured Wark Castle, an English border stronghold near Coldstream. In 1429 we are told that Prior William Drax of Coldingham and others attacked John Colstoun near Cockburnspath, robbed him of 2,000 merks, and took the money to 'Faulst castelle' for safe keeping. In 1431, 1434, and 1438, Thomas and Gilbert de Lumsden are mentioned in connection with the castle. From at least the thirteenth century until 1621 the Lumsden family occupied the lands of Easter Lumsden, now represented by the modern farm of Lumsdaine, to the south-east of Fast Castle.

For reasons which are not entirely clear, no record of the castle survives from the next half-century. Then in 1487 it reappears under the occupation of Sir Patrick Home, the fourth son of the first Lord Home. Sir Patrick was a man of considerable importance, attending several Scottish parliaments, and taking part in negotiations for a number of truces between England and Scotland. During the Home occupation Fast Castle seems to have become a family residence, and it is probably during this period that the castle was in most continuous use. Sir Patrick's status was possibly the reason why Margaret

Tudor, the fourteen year old daughter of Henry VII, lodged at Fast Castle in 1503 on her journey north to Edinburgh to marry King James IV. The Home family welcomed their future Queen into the castle, and we are told that there was 'very good cheer so that every man was content.' Her company of some 1,500 persons, both Scots and English, were put up at Coldingham 'wher was ordonned mett and drynke for them.'

Sir Patrick died in 1509, and his son Cuthbert returned from Turkish service in Cairo to claim his inheritance. He did not however live long to enjoy it, for in September 1513 he was slain at the battle of Flodden. It seems that control of the castle then passed to Alexander, third Lord Home, probably as guardian of Cuthbert's widow and family. Alexander was in conflict with the Regent Albany, who took possession of the castle in 1515. However, the Homes soon regained the castle, although, being unsure of holding it, they made it uninhabitable. A year later Alexander, who had been outlawed by the Regent, was tried for treason and beheaded. In 1521 Alexander's brother George, fourth Lord Home, repaired the castle, which by this time had passed into the keeping of Cuthbert's widow. About 1533 her daughter Elizabeth married Sir Robert Logan of Restalrig, whose main residence was then situated not far from Edinburgh. This union transferred Fast Castle and other Home properties to the Logan family for the remainder of the century. When Sir Robert died ten years later the castle was inherited by his son and heir Robert, the sixth Baron of Restalrig. In 1542 the younger Robert, then about nine years old, married Margaret Seton, daughter of George, sixth Lord Seton. Margaret was a half sister of Marie, one of the 'four Maries' who attended Mary Queen of Scots.

In 1543 a marriage treaty was agreed whereby Edward, the six year old son of King Henry VIII, would marry the infant Mary Queen of Scots when she reached the age of eleven. However, the Scottish parliament broke off the treaty and, during the next seven years, the Border country suffered a series of English invasions in a war known to the Scots as the Rough Wooing. A signalling system to give warning of these incursions stretched from St. Abbs Head to Linlithgow, and in 1547 Robert Logan was made responsible for the 'bailefire' at Dowlaw above Fast Castle. The last attack from the south ended in the same year with the defeat of the Scots at the battle of Pinkie. Fast Castle was then captured and garrisoned by the English, as were the strongholds of Dunglass, Lauder, Eyemouth, Home, and Broughty Crag. During this occupation, in 1549, a plan of the castle was drawn under the direction of Henry, second Earl of Rutland, as Lord Warden of the East and Middle Marches. The plan [Plate 19], one of the earliest to depict any Scottish castle or house, has been invaluable to those concerned with excavations at the site. However, Fast Castle did not remain under English control for long, being recaptured in the winter months of 1549–50. Its captain had called for supplies, which were carried into the castle on the shoulders of the local 'husbandmen', acting under orders from Alexander, fifth Lord Home. Once inside, these bearers slew the gatekeepers, and before the garrison could retaliate the Scots had won the day.

Robert Logan died in 1561 and his second wife, Dame Agnes Gray, then obtained control of the castle, for his son Robert was only six years old. Dame Agnes later married Alexander, Lord Home, who as her husband then had authority over Fast Castle until young Robert came of age. In 1567 Mary Queen of Scots had just been confined in Loch Leven Castle, and Queen Elizabeth's ambassador, Sir Nicholas Throckmorton, was among those present at a meeting held in Fast Castle on 11 July to consider the situation. He wrote to Sir William Cecil, Elizabeth's secretary, that he 'was intretyd very well accordinge to the state of the place, which is fitter to lodge prisoners than folks at lybertye, as yt is very little so yt is very stronge.' Yet the castle's strength did not prevent its capture once again by the English in 1570. Queen Elizabeth, angered that Alexander, fifth Lord Home, had given refuge to the Earl and Countess of Northumberland, who were fugitives from the unsuccessful northern rebellion, ordered that Fast Castle be attacked. On 4 May, according to one source, Sir William Drury marched against the castle at the head of 2,000 men and took it without firing a shot. Although this report may have exaggerated the strength of his force, 200 men perhaps being nearer the truth, an English garrison held the castle until November 1573.

Robert Logan, the seventh and last Baron of Restalrig, great-great-grandson of Sir Patrick Home, came of age in 1576 and thus acquired his inheritance. He is undoubtedly the most notorious of all Fast Castle's owners, his celebrity stemming from a reputed connection with the 'Gowrie Conspiracy' of 1600, and from the previously mentioned contract of 1594 between him and John Napier. The young Sir Robert seems to have quickly acquired a name for involvement in black deeds and political intrigues. For example, in 1593 he was denounced as a rebel after having failed to appear at court to answer 'upoun his treasounable conspyring, consulting, trafficquing, and divising with Frances, sometyme Erll Bothuill.' As the Logans of Restalrig held land in various parts of the country and their main residence was near Edinburgh, Fast Castle must have been rather infrequently used by its owners. Perhaps for long periods, broken by intermittent visits from Sir Robert and his household, only a caretaker or tenant was in occupation. By the time of his death in July 1606 Robert Logan had disposed of all his property, including Fast Castle in 1602. This work deals mainly with the castle's subsequent history.[9]

Facing page: PLATE 3. Scotland from the Moray Firth to the Solway Firth, 1573.

Overleaf: PLATE 4. Buchan to the Borders.

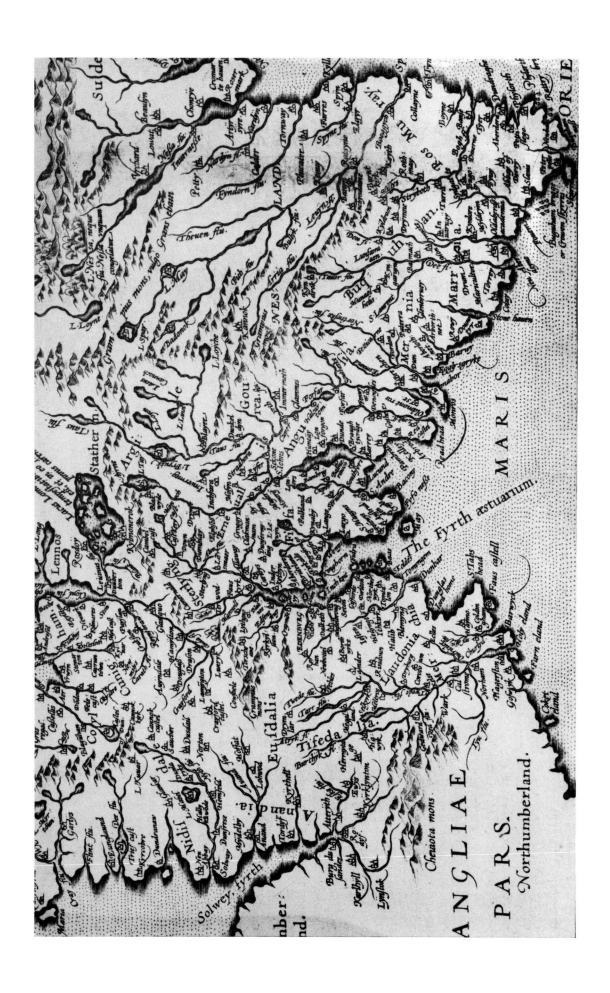

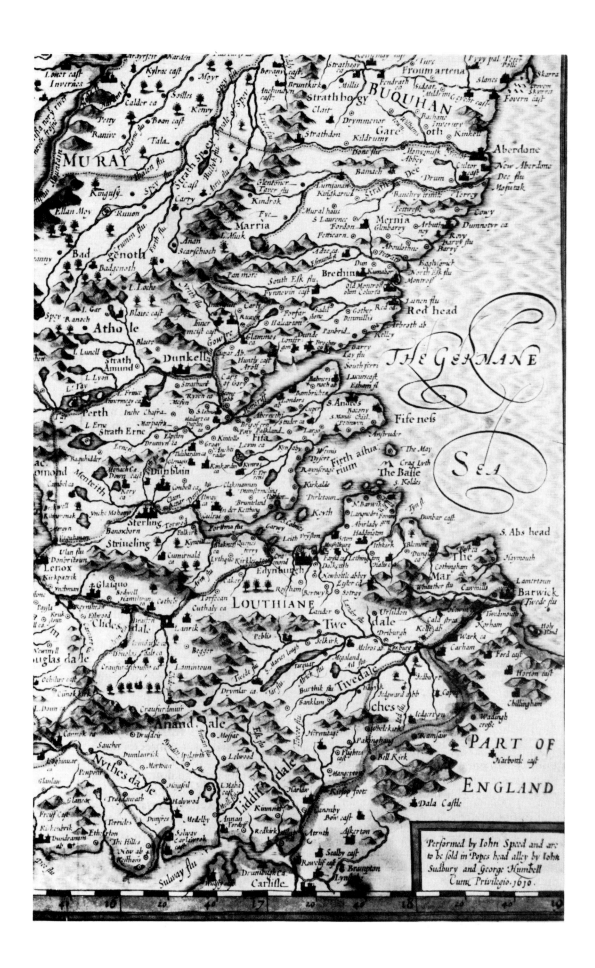

Chapter 1

Logan, Douglas, the Earl of Dunbar, and Arnott

As the seventeenth century began, Fast Castle was entering into the last phase of its useful life, both as a place of residence and a site of strategic importance. Events during the previous 200 years had clearly demonstrated the value of the castle's situation atop its high and craggy promontory. Although attacked and captured on a number of occasions, the castle certainly justified its name. However, a distinct change in the castle's fortunes was on the way. Although another 150 years would pass before rural life in Scotland altered significantly from its late-medieval pattern, national events and trends were making structures such as Fast Castle redundant. The castle was already heading into decline and obsolescence. One aspect of this change, important for our understanding of developments between 1602 and 1682, is the greater instability brought to the castle's ownership and occupation. During the previous 115 years Fast Castle had been the heritable property of only two families: the Homes of Fast Castle and the Logans of Restalrig. After Robert Logan sold the castle and associated lands in 1602, it was to change hands several times over the next eighty years. But although we have a fairly complete list of Fast's owners, we are left very much in the dark as to how long it was actually occupied during this period and, unfortunately, most of the stereotyped legal documents give little indication on the subject. It had been hoped to uncover information which would give some idea of everyday life within the castle walls but, sadly, there is a similar lack of evidence, making any interpretation largely speculative. Indeed, it must be said that the tortuous history of Fast Castle's seventeenth-century ownership is not easy to follow. The reader should however be assured that the worst complexities are confined to Chapters 2 and 3; thereafter the narrative becomes relatively straightforward.

That Fast Castle was considered important, particularly during its heyday in the sixteenth century, is shown by its inclusion on some of the first maps of Scotland. The earliest known map recording the existence of the castle is that published by Abraham Ortelius in 1573 [Plate 3]. On the east coast from Berwick to Dunbar the map only mentions the following places: 'Barwyck, Coldingham, Faus castell, S'Tabs, Dunglas and Dunbar.' Obvious errors occur in this map: for example, Fast Castle is placed south of St. Abbs, while Eyemouth (Haymo) is situated away from the coast and west of Coldingham.[1]

Five years later, in 1578, the Scottish historian and divine, Bishop John Leslie, published his great history of Scotland, and it included a much less accurate map of Scotland than that of Ortelius. In an area roughly bounded by Edinburgh, Kelso, Berwick, and the coastline, just ten places are recorded, one of which is Fast Castle.[2] Our research has covered only a very small percentage of the available maps of Scotland and Great Britain, but sufficient have been studied to observe that the castle is frequently delineated on maps from the seventeenth century onwards. For example, it is to be found on the maps of Scotland and Great Britain produced by John Speed in 1610 [Plate 4].[3] About 1626 the great Dutch publishing house of Willem and Joannis Blaeu began to take an interest in the mapping of Scotland for inclusion in their projected world atlas. By 1645 four volumes had been published, but it was not until 1654 that the counties and regions of Scotland were included in a separate volume. A great deal of the initial surveying for this immense project was undertaken by Timothy Pont between 1585 and 1600. Eventually his surviving manuscripts were sent to Blaeu, and where necessary were corrected and added to by Robert Gordon of Straloch and his brother James. Pont surveyed most of Scotland unaided, but he died long before his efforts were published. Anticipating the circulation of the atlas, Gordon wrote to Sir John Scot in 1648 concerning Pont's work: 'Now at length after many labours, after the loss of much time and after such troubles as the mind shudders to remember, our Scotland is worthily admitted to her place in the great and famous Atlas of Joannes Blaeu.'[4]

The county map of 'The Merce or Shirrefdome of Berwick' [Plate 5] contains a wealth of new information and delineates many of the small farms or settlements not located in earlier surveys. The map is of particular interest as it identifies most of the settlements mentioned in the charters connected with Fast Castle. The only road shown on the map is the old post road from Berwick to Edinburgh, and it gives the impression of being a continuous and uninterrupted highway. This, however, would be an inaccurate interpretation because, from later maps and descriptions of the area, particularly in the vicinity of Coldingham Moor, it is clear that parts of the road were difficult to maintain, being little else than a rough and boggy track.[5] Even today, Coldingham Moor appears to some extent as a barren wilderness. A vivid description of the moor and its contrast with the more fruitful lands around Cockburnspath is to be found in Daniel Defoe's *Tour* published in the 1720s. His feelings on crossing the moor must have been those of many a tired and weary traveller:

> ...we enter upon a most desolate, and, in winter, a most frightful moor for travellers, especially strangers, call'd Condingham, or, to speak properly, Coldingham Moor; upon which, for about eight miles, you see hardly a hedge, or a tree, except in one part, and that at a good distance; nor do you meet with but one house in all the way, and that no house of entertainment; which, we thought, was but a poor reception for Scotland to give her neighbours, who were strangers, at their very first entrance into her bounds.... Having pass'd this desart, which indeed, makes a stranger think Scotland a terrible place, you come down a very steep hill into the Lothians.... From the top of the hill you begin to see that Scotland is not all desart; and the Low Lands, which then show themselves, give you a prospect of a fruitful and pleasant country: As soon as we come down the hill, there is a village call'd Cockburnspeth, vulgarly Cobberspeth, where nature forms a very steep and difficult pass, and where, indeed, a thousand men well furnish'd, and boldly doing there duty, would keep out an army, if there was occasion.[6]

Fast Castle was therefore by no means isolated, lying near this main route from England to Scotland, and less than a mile from the old road from Coldingham

PLATE 5. The Berwickshire coast, north of Eyemouth, showing St. Abbs Head and Fast Castle. Note particularly the settlements of Doula (Dowlaw), Duddohoam, Falabanck, Newtoun, Windylawes, Wr. Lumisdenn and the Mill (of Fast Castle).

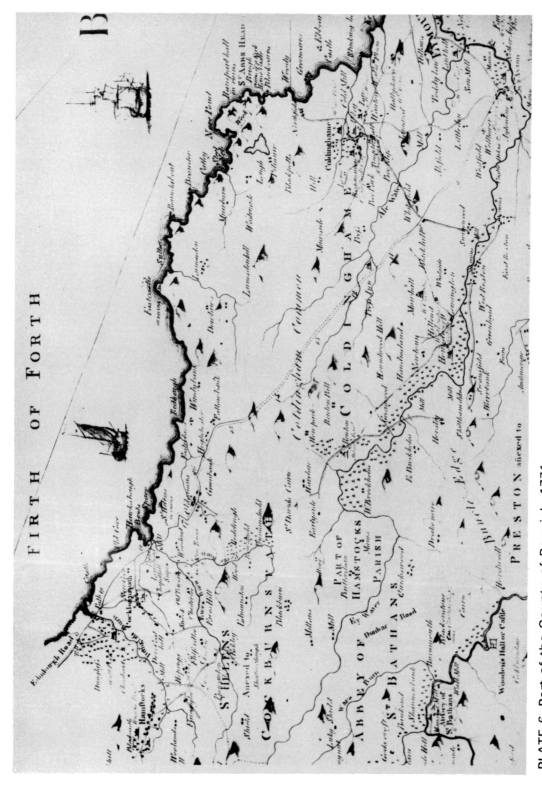

PLATE 6. Part of the County of Berwick, 1771.

through Lumsdaine and Dowlaw.

Before detailing the subsequent history of the castle we must recall that up to the sixteenth century all its lands formed part of the church lands of Coldingham Abbey, and during much of the period under review belonged to the barony of Coldingham. In charters of the late sixteenth century the places specifically associated with Fast Castle are Wester Lummisden, Dowlaw, Duddoholme, otherwise known as Cauldsyde, and the mill of Fast Castle. Two other sites added to this list in legal documents from 1606 are Auldtoun and Newtoun. Prior to the mid-eighteenth century it is impossible to say much about these small settlements, due simply to the lack of information, although there is evidence suggesting that several more existed which were not mentioned in any of the charters. Blaeu shows all of these places except Auldtoun, which nevertheless still survived at the turn of the century. The name Wester Lummisden gives rise to a certain amount of confusion. Some charters refer to the lands of Fast Castle, called Wester Lummisden, Cauldsyde, and Dowlaw, while others mention the lands of Fast Castle or Wester Lummisden, Dowlaw, and Cauldsyde. These differences are presumably accounted for by the fact that there was a settlement called Wester Lumsden, and that the name also served for the lands of Fast Castle in general.

For reasons which are not altogether clear, Robert Logan appears to have sold off all his lands and estates by the time that he died at Edinburgh in July 1606. The dissipation of this valuable and widespread property began almost immediately after Logan came of age in 1576. Lands were sold piece by piece so that by 1602 he was left only with Fast Castle and some holdings in Berwickshire, together with a few properties near Edinburgh, including the barony of Restalrig.[7] In this year Fast Castle's long-standing connection with the Logan family was finally broken. On 10 November 1602 Robert Logan sold the castle and its settlements of 'Wester Lummisden, Cauldsyde and Dowla', together with the mill, mill lands, and fishing rights to Archibald Douglas of Pittendreich.[8]

The contract was confirmed at Edinburgh on 10 August 1605. Unfortunately, it has so far proved difficult to identify accurately this member of the Douglas family. Thomson stated in 1908 that Archibald Douglas of Pittendreich was one of the four natural or illegitimate children of the Regent Morton,[9] but other evidence might seem to contradict this statement. James Douglas, fourth Earl of Morton, was the second son of Sir George Douglas of Pittendreich near Elgin, and he married Elizabeth Douglas, daughter of the third earl, in 1543. During most of the time between 1572 and 1580, James was Regent of Scotland, but in 1581 he was tried for treason and beheaded, a victim of the Maiden. James and his wife Elizabeth are reputed to have had ten children, most of whom died young, while James himself had four natural children. From various sources we are informed that James' second illegitimate son was Archibald, who held the lands of Pittendreich. He married Elizabeth Sutherland, and it is recorded that they had one daughter, Elizabeth.[10] Archibald Douglas, who purchased Fast Castle, was by 1606 married to Alison Home. If he and James' illegitimate son were one and the same, it means that he had married at least twice. Whatever his genealogical position in the Douglas of Pittendreich line, Archibald and his descendants were to become a Border family for many years.

While it is impossible to say how much time Douglas spent at the castle, it is perhaps reasonable to assume that he was in occupation during the years

1602–6. That this was his main or only residence during this period seems to be evident from a charter, dated 5 June 1606 and recorded five days later, when he is referred to as 'Archibald Douglas of Fast Castle.' This charter records that Douglas had purchased the mill of Tofts, called Mersington Mill, in the parish of Eccles near Coldstream. He had bought the mill from James Maitland of Lethington, who was the son of William Maitland of Lethington, the famous Scottish statesman known as Secretary Lethington.[11] Although in later charters Douglas is designated as 'Archibald Douglas of Tofts', it seems that until at least 1612 he may have feued or tenanted Fast Castle from the next superior,[12] the Earl of Dunbar.

A few months before Douglas had bought the Tofts mill, Robert Logan was apparently selling the last of his property. On 4 January 1606 an Extract of Registered Letters of Consent by James, Lord Balmerino, Secretary for Scotland and President of the College of Justice, was recorded. The consent related to the sale by Robert Logan and his wife Marion Ker of their lands of Flemingtoun in the barony of Coldingham to George Home, Earl of Dunbar [Plate 7], but also covered 'the acquisition by the said Earl of the lands of Fastcastle, with the Mains thereof or Wester Lumsden, Dowlaw and Doliolme or Cauldsyde' from Archibald Douglas and his wife Alison Home.[13]

George Home, third son of Alexander Home of Manderston, was a man of considerable prominence and a great favourite of King James VI. Described by Archbishop Spottiswoode as a man of deep wit and few words,[14] George became a member of King James's bedchamber and was knighted in 1590. On 7 July 1604 he was sworn a Privy Councillor of England and created Baron Home of Berwick. On 3 July 1605 he was made Earl of Dunbar, a title which had been unused since 1435.[15] At about the same time he took office as Chancellor of the Exchequer in England. In September 1606, while acting as commissioner for keeping the peace within the Border country, he dealt most effectively with 'the brokin men and forners' of both kingdoms. At two courts held by him, he condemned 'and caussed hange aboue 140 of the nimblest and most pouerfull thieves in all the Borders' who were most obnoxious to the public peace. We are informed that by this action the earl fully reduced the other inhabitants to the obedience of the king's law.[16]

Early in 1606 he and the Earl of Dunfermline[17] were sent from the court to Edinburgh to deal with religious matters. Largely through his efforts the act for the restoration of the estate of bishops was carried through at a parliament held at Perth on 9 July 1606.[18] While thus taking care of both judicial and religious matters George, who had been an earl for one year, was granted a charter of novodamus over the lands of the Earldom of Dunbar. Dated at Whitehall and Perth on 1 and 9 July, the charter has a preamble which describes the earl in glowing terms:

> Inasmuch as we, revolving frequently in our memory the faithful, most profitable, lengthened, and most pleasing obediences and services rendered to us by our most faithful and beloved Kinsman and familiar counsellor George Earl of Dunbar, Lord Home of Berwick, high treasurer of our realm of Scotland, and Chancellor of the Exchequer in England, who having in his earliest youth really dedicated and firmly bestowed all the cares and thoughts of his body and soul, his whole life even to us, and to our safety, service, and most noble will, has continued to this

13

PLATE 7. George Home, Earl of Dunbar, d. 1611.

day with the same constancy and perfect fidelity in this his most noble purpose of deserving well of us.

James goes on to credit George with discovering and combating, successfully and alone, Bothwell's rebellious schemes. Also George's exertions in domestic and foreign diplomacy had paved the way for the king's peaceful accession to the English throne. The extensive lands covered in the charter were those of 'Greenlaw, Reidpeth, Fowlden, Edingtoun, Pincartouns, Lochend, Fastcastell, Flemyntoun, Fairneyside and Lambertoun.'[19]

By an Act of Parliament, all these lands were erected along with other grants into the Earldom of Dunbar, including

> ...other castles, manorplaces, lands, mains, mills, mill lands, multures, fishings, meadows, lochs, links, and all their pertinents, and their teinds included together with the rights of patronages of all parsonages, vicarages, chanonries, prebendaries, chaplinaries and others whatsoever generally and specially mentioned with all their pertinents, tenants, tennendries, pendicles and dependencies in one whole and free earldome, Lordship of parliament and free barony to be called in all time coming the Earldom Lordship Barony of Dunbar.

As superior of all these lands, and so that his infeftment of them might be effectual and perpetually valid, George was required to make a separate yearly payment where necessary for the individual holdings. For example, he was to pay, if asked, a red rose for the barony of Greenlaw, and payment was to be made at the castle of Greenlaw on the feast of St. John the Baptist's birthday. For the lands of Fast Castle, Flemington and Fernyside, the payment was to be 'threscoir pundis scottis money.'[20] Payments such as these were nominal and rarely demanded.

Having the rights of superiority over all these lands must have given George Home considerable control over the lives of his tenants, in what by any standards was a vast land empire. It is perhaps interesting to wonder whether the earl, amidst all his political and personal commitments, had time to visit many of these properties, including Fast Castle's rugged promontory. The Earl of Dunbar returned to London in 1610, and on 20 January 1611[21] he died suddenly at Whitehall, there being some suspicion of poisoning.[22]

On 16 July 1612 Archibald Douglas received a new crown charter for Fast and its associated settlements, his last recorded connection with the castle.[23] It is probable that, soon after obtaining this charter, the Douglas family were completely settled at Tofts. However, it would appear that they were keen to get back to the locality of the castle for, after Archibald died, his son and heir William purchased the lands of Easter Lumsden on 26 May 1621.[24] Lumsden was to remain in the Douglas family until it was sold on 3 July 1685 to Sir Patrick Home of Broombank.[25]

After the Earl of Dunbar's death the superiority and control of the earldom passed to his two daughters, Lady Anne and Lady Elizabeth. Anne was married to James Home of Whiterig near Ayton, while Elizabeth was married to Lord Howard de Walden, later to become Earl of Suffolk.[26] On 16 December 1613 Lady Anne obtained a crown charter, ratifying the purchase of her sister's half of the lands belonging to the earldom, which included Fast Castle and its settlements.[27] The castle is next mentioned in a charter between Lady Anne, with consent of her husband, and Sir Gideon Murray of Elibank or Eliburn in Selkirkshire.[28] The charter was concluded on 12 June 1615 and ratified on 3 April 1618. It designated Anne as Lady Anne Home, Lady Coldingknowes junior. In the charter, Lady Anne granted to Sir Gideon the annual revenue from the lands of the barony of Greenlaw Reidpath, together with the lands of Fast Castle, which amounted to 2,000 merks or some £1333 Scots.[29] This would have equalled £111 sterling, its modern (1987) equivalent being about £4,000. Why these revenues were given to Sir Gideon is unknown, but one possible explanation is that they were pledged to raise money for some form of loan or mortgage. It is unnecessary to go into the biography of Sir Gideon, except to illustrate his association with the Earl of Dunbar and others connected with Fast Castle. In 1607 he was appointed one of the commissioners to assist the Earls of Dunbar and Cumberland in establishing peace on the Borders, and in 1610 he received a pension of £1,200 Scots from the Earl of Dunbar. In 1611 he was appointed, along with others, to manage the king's affairs in Scotland and from 1612, until his death in 1621, he was Treasurer Depute.[30]

In consequence of an agreement between Lady Anne Home and Sir John Arnott of Berswick, dated 11 and 15 December 1615, Fast Castle next came into the possession of his son, James Arnott senior, a merchant burgess of Edinburgh. After Lady Anne had resigned her rights to the castle, James obtained a new grant which was registered on 26 April 1616.[31] Before dealing with James Arnott, we should examine in more detail the history of his father and the Arnott connection with the area.

As early as 1564, John and his parents had purchased the church lands of Auldhamstocks within Cockburnspath called 'the hospital'.[32] By this time John was already a burgess of Edinburgh, having been admitted to the Burgess Roll on 18 August 1561 after payment of 33s 4d Scots. Sir John seems to have been something of a financial wizard, amassing a vast fortune. In 1592 he was elected Provost of Edinburgh, and he again held that honoured post from 1608 till his death in 1616.[33] One result of Sir John's business success was his ability to lend large sums of money to King James, £6,000 in 1594 for example. On this occasion James gave him as security 'ane drinking pece of gold, weyand tuelff pound and fyve unce of gold.' If the money was not repaid, John could melt down the pledge and use the metal to strike five pound pieces of gold.[34] Sir John began to invest his wealth in land purchase. In 1605 he acquired four oxgates of land in Restalrig, and in 1606 he was infefted in his lands in Orkney, whence he took his title of Berswick. This property included the lands and isles of 'Birsay, Sandwick, Hoy, Walles, South ronaldshay, Schappenschaw, Deerness, Sanday, Stronsay, Egilsay, Rowsay and North ronaldshay.'[35]

Later Arnott acquired lands in Cockburnspath, Woodmylne in Fife, and Granton near Edinburgh. Between 1604 and 1611 he held the post of Treasurer Depute, prior to Sir Gideon Murray. While he was acting in this capacity, his name appeared in the Act of Parliament ratifying the Earldom of Dunbar to George Home in 1606. In the preamble it states that 'Sir Johne Arnote of berswik knycht his grace thesaurar depute in place of the said erle being now thesaurar principal himself Gevis grantis heretablie disponis and perpetualie confermis To his said richt trustie and weilbelouit cousing and familiar counsaillor George erle of dunbar' all the lands within the Earldom.[36]

Robert Logan's death in 1606 had made it necessary that arrangements be settled for looking after his children's interests. As a result, disputes arose between Alexander, Earl of Home, their grandmother's second husband, and Marion Ker, Robert Logan's last wife. Alexander apparently wanted to take the children, including Robert, the eldest son and heir, under his care and protection. It was agreed that these issues should be put to arbitration and at Douglas, on 5 August 1606, a document was signed whereby an agreement could be reached. Eight arbiters were selected, four to each side, including Sir John Arnott of Berswick as one of Marion Ker's representatives.[37]

On 12 August 1608 a familiar and grisly scene was enacted in the High Street of Edinburgh, when George Sprot was hanged near to the market cross. Sprot, who was Robert Logan's notary or law agent, had been convicted for reputed involvement in the Gowrie Conspiracy which, one year later, resulted in his client's posthumous forfeiture. At this time Sir John Arnott owned a house opposite the market cross, and he and several other noblemen, including the Earl of Dunbar, watched Sprot's execution from one of the windows.[38] Robert Logan's alleged connection with the Gowrie Conspiracy was to bring about an Act of Parliament in 1609 in favour of Sir John Arnott and several others. The Act declared that they were innocent of 'the horrible and destable treassoun committit aganis hes majesties awin persone', thereby ensuring them peaceable possession of the lands, tacks, teinds and possessions which they had purchased from the late Robert Logan.[39] A few years later, in 1611, Sir John was appointed to the committee of new 'Octavians' to supervise the finance of the kingdom. The committee consisted of eight councillors, one of whom, as has already been pointed out, was Sir Gideon Murray of Elibank.[40] This association establishes yet another personal link with Fast Castle.

According to James Arnott, the main historian of the Arnott family, Sir John Arnott of Berswick was married four times. His first wife was Helen Johnstone, by whom he had three sons and two daughters. His eldest son, John, was given the estate of Woodmylne in Fife, but he predeceased his father. The second son, William, obtained the estate of Cockburnspath, while his third son, James, was given the barony of Granton.[41] James Arnott of Wester Granton married Maddalene Thomson in 1598, and had one daughter, who married John Wilkie of Foulden. On 27 May 1613 he and his wife, together with his father Sir John Arnott, acquired the lands of Wester Granton and, as has already been stated, he purchased Fast Castle in 1615.[42] From the evidence studied so far, it is not possible to give any indication whether James and his family ever occupied the castle. Certainly their main residence was still at Wester Granton as late as 1621, and no documentation has been seen describing James Arnott as 'of Fast Castle'. Like his father, James was a merchant burgess of Edinburgh, and for a time seems to have been prosperous. Perhaps attempting to emulate his father, James undertook a number of public duties. Thus in 1617 he was 'placed on a commission for the plantation of Kirkis'. King James had become concerned that there were many churches without ministers, causing ignorance and atheism to abound among the people. Also many of the churches which had ministers lacked sufficient funds to maintain them. The commission was appointed to look into these matters.[43]

Returning to Cockburnspath, we find the Arnott family having considerable local influence during the first two decades of the seventeenth century. In 1606 Sir John transferred his title of the customs, imposts and anchorages for all goods entering the harbours of 'Quhyitcoif and Gudeschirrisoill' near Cockburnspath to his son William.[44] In 1609 William Arnott obtained a charter over the lands, lordship and barony of Cockburnspath.[45] Later, in 1612, he was allowed to erect the village into a free burgh of barony, with the power to create bailiffs and burgesses, and hold a burgh court and a weekly Wednesday market.[46]

However, time was running out for the Arnotts. William and his brother James suffered severe financial difficulties, resulting in the family's decline into obscurity, with their brother-in-law James Dalziel as the apparent cause. Both brothers went surety for Dalziel, who became bankrupt. In 1621, when William's debts totalled £4,000, he was obliged to sell Cockburnspath for that sum to Thomas Nicolson, commissary of Aberdeen.[47] James' situation in this sad tale seems to have been worse than that of his brother William. On 29 June 1624 the Lords of the Privy Council wrote to King James concerning their enquiries into his bankruptcy. James had been accused of making over part of his estate fraudulently to others in an attempt to escape his creditors, but after an investigation into the matter the Lords proved that this was not the case. James had sold all his property, and paid the debts of James Dalziel to the tune of 'fourscoir and sevin thousand merkis Scottishe money.' James Arnott must have been afraid that enquiries would go against him, as to escape imprisonment he had retired to Berwick, where he seems to have lived in straitened circumstances. The once rich Edinburgh merchant now depended 'upoun the benevolence and charitie of his friendis, and by suche supplie as thair compassionate pitie of his indigent estate enforces thame to minister unto him for the interteynment of his lyff.'[48]

Exactly when James Arnott sold Fast Castle has not been completely established. Alexander Carr, its earliest historian, states that Arnott resigned the castle along with the lands of Wester Lumsden to the Homes on 24 May 1617. Carr cites as his authority 'Papers in the possession of Sir John Hall, Bart.', which would appear to refer to the inventory of evidence relating to Old Cambus and Fast Castle, written about 1682. Unfortunately, the item containing the 1617 date is vague in meaning, and seems to imply that James Arnott resigned the castle on 27 January 1620.[49] On 27 June 1620 a charter was recorded granting Fast Castle and its lands to Lady Marie Sutton, widow in liferent, and in fee to her son James, Earl of Home. Although the charter states that the lands had been resigned by James Arnott, it unfortunately does not give the date of the resignation.[50] However, from a later contract in 1621 there is substantive evidence that Arnott sold Fast Castle to Lady Marie's husband, Alexander, sixth Lord and first Earl of Home. As he died at London on 5 April 1619, this would go some way to validate Carr's resignation date of 1617.

During the next few years the Homes and another local family, the Stewarts of Coldingham, were to be involved in what may be described as a right royal legal battle over the lands and revenues of Fast Castle. The histories of these two rival border families were in many ways closely connected, particularly in relation to the lands of Coldingham. To understand the relevance of their connections with the castle, we first need to examine their associations with Coldingham Abbey.

Chapter 2

The Homes and the Stewarts

Alexander, first Earl of Home, was the son of Alexander, fifth Lord Home, and Dame Agnes Gray, the widow of Robert Logan, the sixth Baron of Restalrig. Through this connection the first earl and Robert Logan, the seventh and last Baron of Restalrig, were half brothers. By 1582 the Earl of Home was discharging his duties as Warden of the East Marches, and on 10 August 1592 King James appointed him as 'the undoubted and irrevocable commendator of the priory and abbacy of Coldingham.' His appointment to this valuable benefice came about through the forfeiture of Francis Stewart, Earl of Bothwell, whose young son John was disqualified from holding that position. Although Alexander's appointment to the benefice was to be for the rest of his life, during the next fourteen years he was only to enjoy the spiritual revenues, the temporal revenues having been annexed to the Crown.[1] In March 1605 Alexander was created Earl of Home and Lord Dunglass, and a year later became Lord Jedburgh and Coldingham. In July 1606, as a reward for services rendered, King James erected the lands which formerly belonged to the Abbeys of Jedburgh and Coldingham into a temporal lordship in favour of the earl, 'to be callit in all tyme cumying the lordschip of Coldinghame.' This included the superiority of the lands within the lordship, together with teinds and rents, all which were to be held from the king, for an annual payment of 400 Scots merks. One of the items, however, which was particularly excepted from this lordship was Fast Castle and its lands, which had been given to George, Earl of Dunbar.[2] On 28 June 1607 Alexander married his second wife, Marie Sutton, eldest daughter of Edward, ninth Lord Dudley. They had four children, James their eldest becoming the second Earl of Home.[3]

To trace the Stewart connection with Fast Castle, we must go back to 1541, when Lord John Stewart was appointed commendator of Coldingham Abbey. In 1562 he married Jean Hepburn, daughter of Patrick, third Earl of Bothwell. John, an illegitimate son of James V, had one legitimate child, his son and heir Francis, and two other illegitimate children. Francis Stewart, Earl of Bothwell, born in 1563, was to become notorious in Scottish history, particularly during the last decade of the sixteenth century, and for some time was an associate of Robert Logan of Restalrig. Falling from the king's favour, and being accused of witchcraft in 1591, he had all his estates and titles forfeited. Francis married Margaret Douglas, a daughter of the seventh Earl of Angus and, according to Balfour Paul, they had eight children.[4] Only three of these children are of relevance to the history of Fast Castle. They are Francis, the eldest son and heir, John, the last commendator of Coldingham, and Harie or Henry, the third child.

On the same day as his forfeiture, Francis made over the estate of Coldingham to his infant son John, presumably hoping to keep it from falling into other hands. If this was the case, the attempt failed for, again on the same day, a Bill of Dishabilitation was passed, disqualifying his infant children from holding any of the titles or lands belonging to their father.[5] The lands of Coldingham, which had thus been taken from Francis and his son John, formed part of the lordship that was given to Alexander, the first Earl of Home.

Apparently there was considerable rivalry and antagonism between the Home and Stewart families, illustrated by King James's involvement as mediator in their differences over the abbacy of Coldingham. The battle for supremacy of the lordship began in 1616 when John Stewart, now grown to manhood, attempted the recovery of his rights over the Coldingham estate by representing to James I, his great uncle, the severity of the Bill of Dishabilitation passed against him. As a result the king ordained that the Earl of Home should sell the lands of Coldingham to John for £4,000, and a yearly income from the estate of £300. Obviously the king's judgement was not obeyed, because four years later, after the death of Alexander, Earl of Home, John Stewart remained at loggerheads with the family. The argument was taken up by the earl's widow, Dame Marie, Countess of Home, and their young son James, the next earl. The king was again asked to mediate, and the articles of agreement which he set out were duly signed by the protagonists on 12 April 1620. The earl and his mother were to sell all their rights in the lands and teinds of the abbey to John Stewart. John, on the other hand, was to give them security for a payment of £48,000 Scots, or £4,000 sterling, to be paid by him within three years, starting at Martinmas 1620. This included the annual revenues of £3,600 Scots, to be paid twice yearly, and John was also to grant leases over the teinds of Old Cambus and Fast Castle to the earl and his mother. The agreement was signed at Whitehall, and King James made known his pleasure that the parties concerned should return to Scotland speedily, so that the matter might be quickly resolved.[6]

Four months later, on 23 August 1620, a letter was sent to the king from the Lords of the Privy Council. They informed him that several meetings had been held with the disputants, together with their lawyers, and the matter had been discussed at very great length. After much deliberation, it was agreed that John Stewart was incapable in his own right of taking part in the transactions. The dispositions by James, Earl of Home, Lord Dunglass, were made in favour of a third party, from whom the earl and his mother were to receive security for their money. A further point of contention, however, was still unresolved, and this involved the lands of Old Cambus and Fast Castle. As the earl and his predecessors had been heritable and kindly possessors of these lands, it was 'instantlie vrged on behalf of the erll, that the landis may be reserued and exceptit out of his dispositioun, and that he may hald the same of your maiestie, ather blenshe or few.' John Stewart strongly opposed this appeal, but it was agreed that King James should have the final decision.[7] The third party concerned in the case turned out to be John's brother, Harie. James and his mother the countess had apparently lost the battle to retain the lands given to Alexander Home in 1606. Agreement was finally reached and, from a copy contract dated 30 March 1621, we learn that James and his mother sold their lands of Coldingham, including Old Cambus and Fast Castle, to Harie Stewart for the previously agreed amount of £48,000 Scots. The sale allowed the Homes to retain the lands and teinds of Northfield, together with the office of bailiery of the barony of Coldingham.[8] On another deed of the same date, John Stewart, now commendator of Coldingham, ratified the sale.

At this point it should be explained that some of the intricacies of seventeenth-century Scottish conveyancing, and the complex nature of their associated legal documents, have proved to be beyond the understanding of those involved with this publication. One such instance centres round the sale of Fast Castle by Dame Marie, Countess of Home, and her son to the Stewarts of Coldingham. All the evidence we have discovered seems to imply that the castle was sold with a lease-back arrangement on the teinds belonging to its lands. The Stewarts and their heirs appear to have obtained the rights of superiority over the castle and its farmlands, and retained these till at least 1658. As the Homes later sold the castle to the Hepburns of Waughton, the implication seems to be that they heritably feued it from the Stewarts. To add to the uncertainty, it is unclear whether the Homes sub-feued the castle, or retained it for their own use.

By an Act of Parliament on 4 August 1621, John Stewart, having 'Continewallie frome his zouthe behaveit himselff' was rehabilitated from the effects of his father's forfeiture. All previous statutes relating to John's personal rights since childhood were cancelled, a measure which had particular relevance to his connection with Coldingham. Having been appointed to the benefice of that priory as commendator, John was required to resign all its associated lands into the hands of King James. These lands, including Fast Castle, were then erected into a temporal lordship, called the barony of Coldingham, and returned to John by a crown charter on 16 October 1621.[9] A few days earlier, Francis Stewart, who should have been heir to his father's estate, received a charter from the king allowing him to retain his property. It made clear, however, that this did not extend to the lands previously held by his father or the Earls of Home.[10] The restoration of the brothers to respectability, as well as some of their former lands, rights, and privileges, must have brought them considerable pleasure and satisfaction. No doubt they savoured what seemed to them a deserved triumph over the Home family. However, John Stewart's good fortune was short-lived because, by an ironic twist of fate and the mismanagement of his affairs, he soon found himself in a financial quagmire leading to complete impoverishment. Indeed it is unclear by what means, apart from the blue blood running through the Stewart veins, John and Harie had managed to acquire the estate of Coldingham.

John appears to have had little head for money matters. This may have been one of the reasons why he was excluded from taking part in the transactions relating to the acquisition of Coldingham, although it should be said that Harie had similar problems. Unable to obtain securities for Harie's first payment to the Earl of Home at Martinmas 1620, both Stewart brothers agreed that the lands should be transferred back to the earl until such time as payment was made. One result of this was that the earl caused a large quantity of the teind corn sheaves from the barony to be thrashed out for his own use. Both he and his mother then sent a warrant to William Craw of Fallabank, instructing him to arrange for the thrashing of the corn standing in Coldingham barnyard. He implemented the command by sending out notices to three individuals, including William Dalyell, an Eyemouth notary. Craw seems to have received quite a shock from the response which these instructions elicited, presumably under instigation by the Stewarts. The three men who had been served notice visited the Homes' agent at his home near Old Cambus, obviously with the purpose of intimidating him. They arrived at the house in a great rage, 'bragging, boasting, threattining, and avowing with mony horribill and fearfull oathes that thay sould not only losse thair lyves, bot thay sould have his lyff, afoir a sheaff of that corne wer cassin in.' Craw took these threats of violence seriously enough to bring the matter before the Lords of the Privy Council although, as he did so more than a year after the event, other factors may have lain behind his complaint.[11]

Harie Stewart's inability to procure guarantors for his first payment to the Earl of Home perhaps becomes more understandable when John's financial position is taken into account. The state of Harie's finances are not known, but it may be surmised that prospective guarantors considered him a bad risk. Certainly, at some time between 1621 and 1622 John Stewart, later described as a worthless and profligate individual, found himself close to bankruptcy. Discovering that his estate was heavily burdened with debt, and wishing to extricate himself and his creditors from this embarrassing situation, John was forced to place most of his property in the hands of William Douglas of Blackerstoun, whom John described as a trusty friend.[12] Precisely how much of the barony of Coldingham was mortgaged to Douglas is uncertain, but some of the evidence suggests that the whole estate, including Fast Castle, had come under his control. According to a complaint made to the Lords of the Privy Council by Robert Douglas in 1630, both he and his father-in-law had been in possession of the lands and rents of Coldingham for the previous ten years without challenge or interruption.[13]

On 16 June 1622 John Stewart sold the barony to his brother Francis, but it is not recorded whether this was a simple family exchange or a deal arising from financial necessity.[14] A year later, on 8 July 1623, a crown charter was granted to the Earl of Home, ratifying to him the annual revenues of the barony, which amounted to £3,600 Scots, and recorded that the revenues for Old Cambus and Fast Castle were valued at £1,200 Scots or £100 sterling. The grant, originally dated 15 May, was made on behalf of Henry (Harie) and John Stewart, with consent of Francis, and also included Alexander Cranstoun of Moreiston, William Douglas of Ivelie and William Douglas of Tofts.[15] As late as 1627 John Stewart was claiming the revenues pertaining to Coldingham Priory, and his power and influence over the barony at this time seem to have been not inconsiderable. In 1626, when granting the lands of Easter Lumsden to Alison Home, the widow of Alexander Douglas of Tofts, John styles himself 'Lord Coldingham, Superior,' in the relevant document.[16] His use of the title 'Lord' seems to confirm the possession of a landed estate, presumably that of the Lordship of Coldingham, which he controlled to some degree till 1643. Nevertheless his description of himself as the lands' 'superior' appears to conflict with other evidence. From the information already presented, it is probable that his brother Francis had obtained the rights of superiority when he purchased the barony in 1622.

Not long after making the grant to Alison Home, John's unceasing extravagances apparently brought him the humiliation of being denounced a rebel for not paying his debts to William Douglas of Blackerstoun. William became donator to the escheat and liferent of John's estate, an archaic legal device whereby the liferent on the property was forfeited. William died soon after, and the monetary disputes were taken up by his son-in-law Robert Douglas, together with Alexander Cranstoun of Moreiston, who had also acquired rights and titles to the lands of Coldingham. John Stewart secured several grants of immunity from the Privy Council in support of his fruitless attempts at redressing the situation, but Douglas and Cranstoun appear to have prolonged the issue to their own advantage. At times the dispute became acrimonious, and on 8 March 1631 Stewart and Douglas were obliged as a result of their bickering to appear before the Privy Council. On this occasion both parties agreed to cease 'all injurious speeches the one aganis the other and not to upbraid others with revylling words, either of tham under pane of twa thowsand merkes, to be uplifted from the contraveeners to his Majesteis use.'[17]

On 4 July 1631 Robert Douglas had recourse to the Privy Council on his own behalf. He complained that the feuars, tacksmen and pensioners of

Coldingham Priory would not pay their proper taxes due to him. The supplication recorded that the assessment had been agreed on at a court held at Eyemouth on 13 October 1630, and related further that 'they will make no payment thereof unless they are compelled.' Their reason for refusing payment is not recorded, but it is quite clear from the long list of people involved that some major dispute was in progress. One reason for this large-scale rebellion may have been that, a short time before, John Stewart and others had entered into a contract with the Earl of Home whereby they obliged themselves to pay the earl £19,200 Scots of past debts. If this was not paid by Martinmas 1632, the earl was to regain possession of the estate. Heading the list of defendants is James, Earl of Home, who owed Douglas £25 for his lands of Northfield and other holdings. There follows Dame Marie, Countess of Home, owing £18 15s for her lands of Auld Cambus, and £22 10s for Fast Castle and Duddoholm. Further down the list we come to Jonet Home, widow of William Craw of Fallabank, owing £6 17s 6d for land in Swinewood. The Privy Council found in Douglas's favour, declaring that they were all to pay their taxes within twenty days.[18] Sir Robert Douglas appears to have died not long afterwards, for on 2 February and 26 April 1632 his daughters Grissil and Elizabeth were served heir to a third part of the lands of Coldingham, including Fast Castle and its settlements.[19]

The extensive debts due to the Earl of Home by 1632 were not paid, and he died shortly after the expiry date. Most of the money then became payable to his successor, James, third Earl of Home. Curiously, the new earl appears to have made little or no effort to claim what was rightfully his, and John Stewart remained in possession of the estate until 1643. Latterly, however, the benefits which Stewart could have derived from it must have been seriously curtailed. In 1641 his wife Margaret Home, 'Lady Coldingham', was appealing to the Lords of Council for sustenance, and she seems to have made out a good case, for they instructed Sir Robert Douglas to assign her the teindsheaves of the barony. This provided for both Margaret and her children, but no reference was made to John! Nevertheless by 1643 Margaret's plight had become desperate. A further appeal to parliament recorded that both mother and children were in great distress and misery.[20] John Stewart's eventual fate has not been discovered, but in 1649 the incessant demands of his creditors continued. He was arrested and imprisoned for eight days in the Canongate Tolbooth, and reduced to the point of starvation. After his release John Stewart more or less disappears from the historical record.[21]

Before completing this summary of the lordship and barony of Coldingham, it must be noticed that one important aspect of its ownership has defied all our attempts at interpretation. The problem arises from apparent inconsistencies in the documentary evidence, which give the impression that the property was in the possession of more than one person or family at the same time. Presumably this was not in fact the case, and the difficulty comes either from our failure to find crucial evidence, or from our inexperience in historical analysis. To avoid further confusion, I will present the material as we have found it and leave others to clarify the position.

Sir John Home of Manderston, laying claim to the lordship of Coldingham during the 1740s, stated that in 1643 the Earl of Home took possession of the estate, while in 1698 Brigadier Francis Stewart conveyed it to Sir Patrick Home, his nearest relation. In the preamble to his claim, Sir John commented that the disputes over the lordship were 'of the longest dependence and most expensive of any that was ever before the Court of Session.' Thus the conflict which started with John Stewart and Alexander, first Earl of Home, was still being fought more than a century later.

On the other hand, we must take into account the information contained in a precept or instruction given by Oliver Cromwell on 10 August 1658 relating to all the lands within the barony of Coldingham, including Fast Castle and its settlements. The document concerned was sent to the Sheriff of Berwick, directing him to infeft the barony into the hands of Alexander Home, the eldest legitimate son of Sir John Home of Renton. The precept gives a long list of the lands within the barony, and covers such items as ports and havens, crofts, mills, fishing rights, annual rents, and all teinds, belonging to Coldingham Priory. In summarising Coldingham's recent history of ownership, the precept of infeftment relates that all the foregoing lands, rights and privileges had been erected into a free temporal barony which had been given under the Great Seal to the late John Stewart in 1621. After passing into the hands of Francis Stewart in 1622, the barony next devolved on Robert Stewart as heir to his father, and to his eldest brother Charles. On 26 November 1656 Robert had the barony taken from him for debts due to his cousin by marriage, Harry Home, the illegitimate son of Sir John Home. This transaction, however, kept the barony within the same family, Sir John being married to Margaret Stewart, the daughter of John Stewart, the last commendator of Coldingham. Harry Home then transferred his rights over the barony to his half-brother Alexander, for whom the precept of infeftment was issued.[22]

We may conclude this part of our narrative with one last piece of evidence, which harks back to the contract concluded by the Stewarts and their associates with the Earl of Home in 1623. On 10 November 1665 Dame Elizabeth Douglas, wife of Sir Robert Sinclair of Longformacus, conveyed all her rights to the lands and barony of Coldingham, which had belonged to her grandfather, William Douglas of Ivelie. These were all the lands which belonged to Coldingham Priory, with the mains of Fast Castle or Wester Lumsden, Dowlaw and Duddoholme, and the teinds of the kirks of Coldingham, Ayton, Fishwick, Old Cambus and others. These rights she conveyed to William, Lord Mordington. On the same date James, Earl of Home, conveyed similar rights over the same lands to Mordington.[23]

Chapter 3

The Hepburns and the Ramsays

For the circumstances in which Fast Castle itself finally passed from the Homes' ownership we must return to the family's early seventeenth-century history. James, second Earl of Home, had married his first wife Catherine Carey, eldest daughter of Henry, first Viscount Falkland, in 1622. Their marriage lasted only four years until her death in 1626. He then married Grace Jane, daughter of Francis, first Earl of Westmoreland. James seems to have had a desire to take up residence in England, and in 1631 he went to London, apparently to participate in the activities of the Court. The expense of living in the metropolis appears to have been a source of concern to the earl, as he made frequent requests for money to be sent up from Scotland. On one occasion his mother personally brought him what must have been a large and heavy purse, containing gold coins to the value of £1,244 13s 4d. Two days previously, James had received from another messenger £2,229 6s 8d, also in gold, made up of twelve pound pieces or Units and Double Angels.[1] He was given little time to make his mark on society, for he died at Apethorpe, near Leicester, in 1633. As the earl had no children, his death brought about the extinction of the direct male line of descent from Alexander, first Lord Home.[2]

The Earldom of Home next devolved on James Home, eldest lawful son of Sir James Home of Whitrig. On 22 March 1633 he was served heir to the deceased James, Earl of Home, but because of legal entanglements he did not receive the royal patent to the earldom until 22 May 1636.[3] After the second earl's death his mother the countess was in dispute with family members and others interested in the Home estate. Once more she appealed to the king, this time Charles I, and again Old Cambus and Fast Castle seem to have been at the root of the problem. On 5 May 1635 Charles wrote to the Court of Session instructing that she should not be impeded in her access to law for her rents of the 'Lands of Bergum, Lithin and Kellie'. The law was also to assist the countess in securing her possession of 'the tythes of Fals Castell and Auld Cambesse', in the event that John Stewart of Coldingham should recover them due to the earl having no surviving male heirs.[4] This continuing dispute arose from the default clause forming one of the conditions between the Earl of Home, his mother, and John Stewart, over the lands of Coldingham in 1620.

James, third Earl of Home, married Jean Douglas, a daughter of William, Earl of Morton. At the Hirsel on 13 July 1640 he granted to his wife the countess, in terms of his marriage contract, the liferent of the lands and baronies of Dunglass, Old Cambus, and Fast Castle.[5] This is the first known documentary reference to Fast Castle as a separate barony. James was finally served heir to the lands of Old Cambus and Fast Castle on 1 July 1641.[6] Some eight months later, on 11 February 1642, he obtained the legal instrument of sasine over these lands, including the Old Cambus settlements of 'Windilawes, pyperden, and Reidcheuches.'[7]

In 1642 several creditors had been granted charters to the lands of Coldingham, including Fast Castle, apparently as a result of debts incurred by John Stewart. The first of these charters was granted to 'Thome Craig' on 15

January for 7,455 merks.[8] The next was to Archibald Thomson, a burgess of Edinburgh, and his son James, recorded on 5 February 1642 for 7,268 merks.[9] On 13 June this was followed by a further charter, for 3,085 merks, on behalf of Alexander Home, son of Patrick Home of Ayton, and Margaret Hepburn his wife.[10]

In the midst of these transactions, Old Cambus and Fast Castle were purchased by Sir Patrick Hepburn of Waughton and his son George. The process of transferring the castle to the Hepburns was initiated some time before 9 July 1642, when an extract of the conveyance recorded that the sale was granted by 'James Earle of Home in favoures of Sir Patrick Hepburne of Wauchtone in lyfrent and George Hepburne his second son in fie.' [Plate 8] This was followed by a charter confirming the purchase and included a reservation on behalf of 'Marie Countesse of Home for her lyfrent of the lands.'[11] The sale was finally recorded in the Register of the Great Seal on 22 August 1642.[12] At this time the feu-duty for Fast Castle was £13, while that for Old Cambus was £20. During the first twenty years of the seventeenth century the duty payable for the castle appears to have remained fairly constant at about £30. Thus by 1642 the duty had been more than halved, suggesting either that land values in general had dropped, or that Fast Castle and its settlements had deteriorated, for some unspecified reasons.

The Hepburns of Waughton were a family of longstanding importance in Haddingtonshire, and their family residence was situated near East Linton. About the time that he purchased Fast Castle, Sir Patrick Hepburn was nominated a Privy Councillor of Scotland.[13] Sir Patrick had at least three sons: Sir James, his heir, who was killed while fighting in France in 1637, George, who seems to have died sometime between 1642 and 1646, and John, who succeeded him.[14] As well as Fast Castle, Sir Patrick obtained possession of the township and lands of Old Cambus in 1642.[15] In the same year, on 29 September, a further appraisal on the lands of Coldingham, including Fast Castle, was granted to Sara Millar, widow of Thomas Fleming of Longhermeston, for 8,657 merks.[16]

The Home family's wish to retain a hold on Fast Castle seems to have bordered on an obsession. In 1644 James, the third Earl, is recorded as having violently dispossessed Sir Patrick Hepburn of the lands of Fast Castle and Wester Lumsden. It is not clear what form this violence took, or how long James remained in possession, but he was apparently fined £20,000 Scots for his actions.[17] Similarly, we do not know when Sir Patrick regained control of the castle, but he appears to have resigned his rights over it sometime between 1644 and 1646, probably to his son and heir John. On 5 August 1646 John Hepburn and his wife Marie Ros were jointly infefted in the barony of Waughton, which included lands in Athelstaneford, Cockburnspath, and East Fortune. Fast Castle and its settlements were now incorporated into the lands of Waughton, which had been erected into a free barony.[18] Sir Patrick Hepburn died about this time, for John was served heir to him on 9 November 1649.[19]

Among all the documents generated by complexities of ownership, very little indication is given about Fast Castle's contemporary function and importance. During the early seventeenth century it features in government

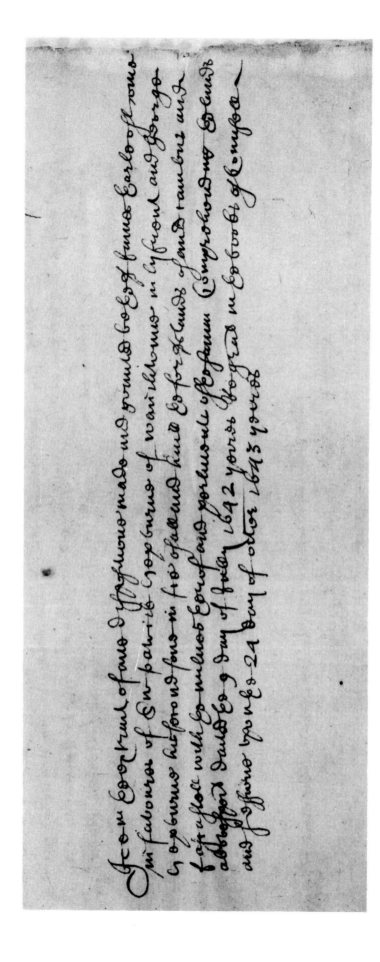

PLATE 8. Extract from Inventory of Writs on Fast Castle, c. 1682: 'Item the extract of ane dispositione made and granted be the fsd James Earle of Home in favoures of Sir Patrick Hepburne of Wauchtoune in lyfrent and George Hepburne his second sone in fie of all and haill the forsd lands of auldcambus and fascastell with the milnes thereof and pertinents of the samin Comprehending the lands abovespeit daited the 9 day of jully 1642 yeires Regrat in the books of Counsell and sessione upon the 24 day of octer 1643 yeires.'

PLATE 9. Sir Andrew Ramsay of Abbottshall, Kt., c. 1620–1688. Provost, latterly first Lord Provost, of Edinburgh.

records as a place near one of the beacons or bale-fires that were still maintained to give warning of foreign invasion.

For example, when Charles I succeeded to the throne in March 1625, Great Britain was on the brink of open hostilities with Spain, largely through the failure of marriage negotiations between Charles and the Infanta Maria. On 8 September he concluded a treaty with the Netherlands against Spain, and early in October a fleet of eighty ships carrying 10,000 men set sail from Plymouth to attack Cadiz. The expedition proved a complete disaster for the British who, after a series of farcical blunders, were obliged to return without having achieved anything. In response to these events the Lords of the Privy Council of Scotland, having been advised that there were 'grite praeparationis of men and armes in divers pairtis of Europe', gave orders on 8 November that precautions be taken against invasion. All His Majesty's subjects between the ages of sixteen and sixty years within the bounds of Edinburgh, Haddington, Berwick, Roxburgh, Selkirk, Peebles, and Linlithgow, were to make themselves ready 'with jakkis, speiris, corslettis, pikis, lang hacquebuttis, and suche other armour as possibilie thay may haif.' They were to go either to Edinburgh or to such parts of the south coast of the River Forth where the enemy appeared. To warn the people when danger was approaching, beacons were to be lit at Edinburgh Castle, North Berwick Law, Garleton Hill, the hill above Fast Castle, and the hill above Ayton, as well as on the Lomond Hills and Largo Law in Fife. At the same time, the Council ordained that letters were to be sent to certain individuals who were appointed to look after the beacons, directing them to appear before the Lords for instructions. On this occasion the Homes' agent William Craw of Fallabank was given the responsibility for maintaining the Fast Castle beacon.

Three days later the Lords were informed that 'Sorle McDonald, assisted and accompanied with a nomber of wear shippis, weill provydit with men and armour, is loused from Dunkirk', at that time under Spanish control, apparently to invade part of the Western Isles. On 12 November the persons who had charge of the beacons appeared before the Privy Council and agreed to prepare them at any sign of danger. It was also agreed that when any of them were alerted to an apparent danger, those concerned would send a man on horseback to the next beacon so that it might be lit. Rather curiously, however, William Craw's name does not appear on the list of persons who were summoned before the Lords, even though these individuals were cited to appear under the penalty of being declared rebels. On the same day Edinburgh Castle was ordered to be provisioned with victuals so that it might 'be the better praeparit for persute or defence upoun everie interveneing occasioun.' A letter was also sent from the Council to King Charles informing him of the scarcity of gunpowder, and requested permission to import it from England. Precisely what threat the Spaniards posed to Scotland's south-east coast, and the scale of their attacks, have not been determined. It is possible that the beacon system was used at least once, for on 29 November the Edinburgh magistrates were ordered to arrange the removal of the hull of a burnt Dunkirk ship from near the mouth of Leith harbour.[20]

By 1627 Great Britain was also at war with France, and on 7 June of that year the Privy Council again ordered that the beacons be prepared for action. The Lords had received a report that William Simson, a burgess of Dysart, on his way home from the Low Countries, was chased by a Dunkirk vessel. 'William so couragiouslie stood to his defence as in a shairp conflict betuixt thame he, to the credit of the natioun, sanke the Dunkirker.' At the same time the Council wrote to the burghs, requesting information on the quantity of gunpowder they had in their possession. During this current emergency, the beacon system was to be greatly expanded and prepared for use. As well as those employed in 1625, Dundee Law, Garriock, Benachie, and Mormond Hill near Fraserburgh, were to be added. The preparation of the Fast Castle beacon now became the responsibility of James, Earl of Home, but we have no indication if the beacons were brought into operation on this occasion.[21]

History does not record the exact position of the bale-fire near Fast Castle, except to say that it was on the hill above the castle. If we take this at face value, the hill referred to must either be Hawksheugh, directly adjacent to the castle, or the much higher Telegraph Hill near to Dowlaw Farm cottages. However, several other possibilities exist, including Lowries Knowes beside the old mill pond at Dowlaw. Of these, perhaps Telegraph Hill would be the most suitable location for the beacon. As late as the Napoleonic wars, a signalling post was located on the hill above the cottages, probably on the site of the old bale-fire.

Fast Castle is mentioned by some of the early seventeenth-century descriptions or guide books of Scotland. The 1607 edition of Camden's *Britannia* makes a summary reference in Latin: 'Invicinia est Fast castle Humiorum castrum a firmitate ita nominatum.'[22] The 1610 edition translates this as: 'Hardby is Fast-castle, a castle of the Lords Humes; so called, for their firmenesse and strength thereof.'[23] On a small point of historical inaccuracy, the 1695 edition had not been updated to show that Fast Castle was by this time the property of Sir John Hall of Dunglass, but still referred to it as belonging to the Homes.[24] As late as 1821 this misleading information was still being incorporated into descriptions of the area by several unwary authorities. Another guide book published in 1612 purported to be 'A true description and division of the whole realme of Scotland, of the situation, distance, and commoditie in every part thereof.' In describing part of Berwickshire it stated that

> South-west from Barwicke lies the towne of Duns, the towne of Langton with castle, the Abbeys of Coldstream and Eccles demolished, the castles of Craighame, the Earl of Homes principal residence, and Wedderburne, [as well as] the very strong Castle of Fastcastle. The riuers in the Mers are Ei, Whiteitur, Blackitur, and Ednam water. This countrey is plenteous and abundant in all things necessary for the vse of man.[25]

William Douglas, in his article on Fast Castle, states that 'in Blaeu's Atlas of 1645, there is a map of Mercia on which the castle is represented by a drawing of a conventional four-sided building. This is only interesting as an indication that it was in occupation at that time.' Although partly correct in his observation, Douglas was mistaken about the date. He appears to have taken his information from Thomson's plate of Blaeu's map published in 1908, which also gives the erroneous date of 1645. As has already been shown, Blaeu's map of *The Merce* was in fact the work of Timothy Pont, surveyed at some time from about 1585 to 1600, and published in 1654. It therefore follows that the castle as depicted on the map probably reflects its existence and occupation during the last fifteen years of the sixteenth century.[26]

The last notable episode in Fast Castle's recorded history took place in 1651, when it was given up to Cromwell's troops. The sequence of events preceding its surrender began on 25 July 1650, when Oliver Cromwell marched into Scotland with 16,000 men and 5,000 horse. A contemporary tract stated that the march from Mordington to Cockburnspath failed to make any contact with the enemy. Instead, as it relates, the troops saw only 'Scotch women' in the places they passed through, 'pitifull sorry creatures, clothed in white Flannell in a very homely manner, very many of them much bemoaned their husbands, who they said were enforced by the Lairds of the Towns to gange to the muster.' On arrival at Cockburnspath, Cromwell was quartered in the house of Sir James Nicholson. When the army scouts first entered the village, they came across only three men, whom they disarmed and made prisoner. Later that night, however, these captives had their swords returned to them by the orders of Cromwell, who the next day marched on with his army to Dunbar and Haddington.[27]

On 3 September the Scottish army suffered ignominious defeat at the battle of Dunbar, with disastrous consequences for Scotland. One immediate result was the surrender of Edinburgh and Leith, except the castle, which held out for several months more. Another was the neutralisation of several 'strongholds' in East Lothian and Berwickshire. The English army report which records their evacuation by the Scots simply lists them as the castles of Dunglas, Hailes, and Hume, along with Fast Castle and Coldingham Abbey. Regrettably the report gives no other details, and we have been unable to determine if these sites were abandoned by civilians or soldiers. Directly after Edinburgh's capitulation, David Leslie, the Scottish commander, withdrew with the remnants of his army to Stirling, where the Committee of Estates and the Commission of the Church were assembled. Cromwell then attempted to capture Stirling, but was defeated by the strength of its fortifications. In December Edinburgh Castle finally surrendered, but on 1 January 1651 Charles II was crowned King at Scone, with the aim of uniting all parties under his standard. During the course of the winter months, Cromwell spent much of his time subduing the country south of the Forth and Clyde. One by one, places such as Roslin, Tantallon, Hume, and Fast Castle, finally surrendered and came under Cromwell's control.

The chronology of events leading up to Fast Castle's capture are recorded quite fully in contemporary news-sheets. The first we hear of the castle is through an entry of *Mercurius Politicus* in the issue Thursday 6-13 February concerning the surrender of Hume Castle. It related that 'this day, Col. Fenwick is come to us, and gives us the glad Tydings of the surrender of Hume Castle sent to him. It is a very seasonable mercy, and will be occasion of much security on the Road to Berwick. I beleeve we shall attempt other places, as Timptallon, and Fance-Castle, that we may be altogether freed from such Back friends.'[28] Two weeks later the paper told its readers of the fall of Tantallon Castle:

Yesterday [21 March], Timptallon Castle was surrendered to Col. Monke, who had laine before it, from Monday was sevennight, and had with him part of Col. Aldridg's, with Col. Sexbys, and Col. Sylers Regiments.... It is conceived the taking of this place will in time necessitate the Bass Island to yeild, the only entrance thereunto being open to it. There is now only remaining between this and Berwick a little place called Faus Castle, which stands into the Sea, & is strong though of little importance, being not able to shelter horse; however, for making clear work it will be summoned.[29]

The following week a rival news-sheet, *The Weekly Intelligencer,* gave a similar report, but described Fast Castle as 'a little hold called Fans Castle which browes into the Sea. It is a strong place, but being not able to shelter any Horse, nor many Foot, it is conceived to be but of little Importance.'[30] On Friday 7 March 1651 readers of the *Intelligencer* learned of Fast Castle's capture: 'The Post this day from Scotland did first of all bring the News to London of the surrender of Fans Castle in Scotland. Upon the first summons, Articles were agreed upon for the surrender of it. It was the last and the least of all the Garrisons which the Scots had on the South of Fife and Sterling, so that now the South of Scotland as farre as Fife and Sterling, is clear to the English army.'[31] From this information we can establish that Fast Castle's capitulation must have occurred on or about 4 March. Taking into account the poor state of the roads, it is remarkable that in the mid-seventeenth century only three days were allowed for the delivery of post between Edinburgh and London. As late as 1816 mail between the two cities was expected to take twelve hours longer than this.[32]

One rather doubtful point in the English descriptions is the statement that the castle could not shelter any horse. From the fragmentary ruins of the entrance complex which remain, it is difficult to determine whether or not horses could gain access. Certainly, from the 1549 plan and the existing foundations, the entrance seems almost too narrow for even a small horse to get into the castle. However, it is likely that horses or ponies were used to transport at least higher-ranking individuals to and from the castle, as the hill climb to Dowlaw would have been very tiresome on foot. Excavations within the inner lower courtyard midden have produced pieces of several horseshoes. Although this evidence is not conclusive, it suggests the use of horses or ponies in the castle's vicinity. Even if it was impossible to shelter these animals inside, a small number could easily have been stabled near the castle's entrance on the mainland, although no evidence indicating such a structure has been observed.

When Cromwell's army was approaching Scotland in 1650, Sir James Nicolson of Cockburnspath left his home, and travelled to Dundee and Edinburgh. He left instructions that some of his valuables should be sent to Fast Castle, presumably for safekeeping. In his 'Diurnal' Sir James records on 25 October 1651, 'compt be Ja Taitt since July 1650...for the paks in fastcastell 1 li 4s.' The valuables were safely returned to Sir James, for on 6 January 1652 the account with Tait records: '...when the trunks wes gottin out of the castel, to William Johnstone 1 li 4s.'[33] It is worth noting that, if these goods were in the castle when it was surrendered in 1651, they had not been taken by Cromwell's troops.

On 27 April 1655 John Hepburn of Waughton granted a bond and disposition containing a precept of sasine to his only daughter, Margaret. The disposition amongst other things covered the annual rent of 1,200 merks, being the interest on 20,000 merks collectable from the lands and barony of Old Cambus and Fast Castle. The bond was confirmed by Oliver Cromwell on 29 June.[34] The fact that John conveyed the annual rent of Old Cambus and Fast Castle to his daughter would seem, along with further evidence, to suggest that there were financial problems in the family. On the same day that the bond was recorded, the barony of Waughton including Old Cambus and Fast Castle was mortgaged to George Norvell, advocate, for the sum of 2,450 merks.[35] A few days later, on 6 July, a bond of corroboration was recorded whereby John Hepburn bound himself to infeft Helen, Isabel and David

Aikinheads in a portion of his lands. These were the lands of Penmanshiel occupied by James Craw, and the lands of Redheugh and Townhead of Old Cambus occupied by Andrew Hepburn.[36] Another mortgage was granted on 6 July to William Hog, advocate, and his wife Katherine Sympsone. This further mortgage by Sir John was over the baronies of Fast Castle and Old Cambus, together with other property in the Constabulary of Haddington. The sum involved on this occasion was 13,317 merks, and 686 merks for payment to the sheriff.[37] Whatever ailed the Hepburn finances, John appears to have partially resolved the situation. He continued in ownership of the barony of Waughton for another fifteen years, although Fast Castle and Old Cambus were still under mortgage to Norvell and the other creditors of Sir John when they were sold in 1670.

Sir John Hepburn died some time prior to 27 August 1669, when his will was recorded in the Edinburgh Register of Testaments.[38] Notice of his death, along with those of several other East Lothian landholders who had been Commissioners of Excise and Justices of the Peace, was recorded on 1 March 1670 by the Lords of the Privy Council. At the same time the Council agreed that 'some fitt persons be appoynted in their places.' Eight new men were nominated, including Sir Andrew Ramsay, Provost of Edinburgh [Plate 9].[39] Apparently before Sir John died, his daughter Margaret had married Sir Andrew Ramsay jnr. of Abbotshall. The date of their marriage has not been discovered, but taking their ages into account it must have been sometime between 1662 and 23 June 1668, by which time their union is recorded.[40]

Great care must be taken in interpreting the Ramsay connection with Waughton, as several previous writers on the families confuse biographical details. Sir Andrew Ramsay of Abbotshall in Fife was a son of Andrew Ramsay, a rector of Edinburgh College and a minister of Greyfriars Church. Sir Andrew had been a merchant and became a bailie of Edinburgh during Cromwell's government. Having purchased Abbotshall from the Scots of Balwearie about 1650, Sir Andrew became Provost of Edinburgh in 1655 and held that office till 1658. He was re-elected in 1662 and in 1667 became the first to bear the title of Lord Provost, a post which he held till 1673. Of all Edinburgh's Lord Provosts, Ramsay has the most unsavoury reputation, from his length of service and to the corrupt practices in which he was involved. Some attempts were made to remove him from office but, these having failed, in 1671 he became a Privy Councillor and a Lord of Session, with the title of Lord Abbotshall. This appointment does not appear to have been well received by his brother lords for, not having been a lawyer by profession, he was, according to Sir George Mackenzie, 'the object of all men's contempt.' In 1685 another attempt was made to re-elect him as Lord Provost but, having failed to win support, Sir Andrew disappeared from Edinburgh's history.

Ramsay married Janet Craw probably at some time in the 1640s, and they had at least one child, Sir Andrew jnr., who was baptised on 24 December 1648. After marrying Margaret Hepburn, the young Sir Andrew, at the age of twenty one, was created a baronet on 23 June 1669.[41] From 1669 till 1674 he represented North Berwick as a Member of Parliament. The alliance between the Ramsays and the Hepburns did not last very long, for Margaret appears to have died sometime during the early 1670s. Their brief union was blessed with at least one son, also called Andrew, who was to become the second baronet. Sir Andrew married secondly Lady Anna Montgomerie, a daughter of Hugh, Earl of Eglinton. Their marriage contract dated 30 December 1675 provided that Anna was to be paid a yearly annuity of 5,500 merks from the revenues of the baronies of Waughton, Abbotshall, Old Cambus and others, presumably including Fast Castle.[42] As John Hepburn's mother-in-law, Margaret Ross was the step-mother of Lady Anna's father, both Hepburn and Andrew Ramsay were connected by marriage to the Montgomeries of Eglinton.

The first record of a Ramsay connection with Fast Castle appears in a disposition dated at the Hirsel and Edinburgh on 16 and 22 July, and 10 August 1670. This conveyed to Sir Andrew Ramsay of Abbotshall, described as 'proveist of Edbro', the lands and barony of 'Auldcambus and fascastell', from Jean, Countess of Home, liferentrix of these lands. Also disposing of their interest in the barony was Jean's son Alexander, Earl of Home, James, Earl of Annandale, and William, Lord Mordington. At the same time, on 21 July, the countess and the others resigned their rights to the barony. Along with the resignation were other dispositions by the previously mentioned George Norvell, advocate, and the other creditors of John Hepburn. A few days later, on 31 July, Sir Andrew Ramsay of Abbotshall received a grant over the lands of Fast Castle, Old Cambus and Waughton, which was recorded in the General Register of Sasines at Edinburgh.[43]

The fact that it was the baronet's father who had acquired these lands may have given rise to the error made by several authors, that it was he who had married Margaret Hepburn, the heiress of Waughton. By the time that Sir Andrew married Anna Montgomerie in 1675, he was designated as of Waughton, clearly separating him from the title of his father. About this time financial arrangements seem to have been made between father and son, whereby control of the barony of Waughton passed to the baronet. He did not however live long to enjoy the benefits of his lands, as he probably died between 1678 and 1680.[44] His son, the second baronet, was served heir on 19 May 1680. Not only did he inherit Waughton, including the lands and barony of Old Cambus and Fast Castle, but he also acquired Abbotshall, which had been the property of his grandfather.[45] The fact that Abbotshall was not co-joined with Waughton appears to stem from a resignation on 30 March 1677, whereby Sir Andrew Ramsay snr. relinquished most of his rights to Abbotshall, Old Cambus and Waughton to his son. This appears to have been brought about in consequence of large debts due to the first baronet by his father.[46]

Although the new laird of Waughton was now possessed of a considerable landed estate, he was only a young boy and not in a position to manage it. The exact date of his birth is not known, but it would appear to have been sometime between 1668 and 1673, so that he was aged between seven and twelve when served heir in 1680. As Sir Andrew's youth required someone to take charge of his affairs, his grandfather was appointed as his tutor at law or guardian. Acting in this capacity, Sir Andrew entered into an agreement on 3 May 1682 with John Hall over the sale of the lands of Old Cambus and Fast Castle.[47] This agreement was shortly to lead to a complete stabilisation of these properties' ownership, which would last into the twentieth century. On 2 June 1682 the sale was completed, but now included the lands and barony of Waughton, all for the purchase price of 121,000 merks. The instrument of sasine for this estate was granted on 29 and 30 August 1682, and registered in the General Register of Sasines on 6 September.[48]

Chapter 4

The Halls of Dunglass

Like his contemporary Sir Andrew Ramsay, John Hall was a wealthy merchant who, by his skill in money-making, reaped considerable rewards both in landed property and political prominence. Hall's official honours included a baronetcy, conferred on 8 October 1687, which originated the long line of the baronets of Dunglass.[1] Sir John's origins are masked in obscurity, but there is some evidence to suggest that his family came from the area of Dunglass. He appears to have been married at least twice, his first wife being Agnes Scott, daughter of John Scott, a goldsmith. They were married on 4 September 1656 and had at least five children, all of whom died young. It was through Agnes that Sir John became a burgess of Edinburgh on 4 March 1657. She died in 1667, and on 17 December 1668 Hall married Catherine Loch of Drylaw, near Edinburgh, widow of John Mein. By Catherine he had at least four children, including his son and heir, James, and William of Whitehall.[2]

On 8 November 1687, a month after receiving the baronetcy, Sir John was granted a charter over the lands of Old Cambus, Fast Castle, Waughton and Dunglass.[3] This grant included various privileges, such as the right to quarry limestone from the barony of Thornton, and to obtain fuel and thatch divots from 'the mure called Chirnside Common.' The bounds of Dunglass estate were completed on 7 July 1694, when the Privy Council approved Sir John's purchase of Cockburnspath by means of a roup or public auction. It cost Sir John £82,000 Scots to buy Cockburnspath from the bankrupt estate of William and John Nicolson, and it seems that he paid over the odds to acquire it.[4] By 1687 Sir John was not only a baronet but a privy councillor, and in April 1689 became the second Lord Provost of Edinburgh to own Fast Castle. He resigned this office two years later, saying that he would have done so at the past election 'had it not been the desire of certain persones to thrust him off without his consent.' He was re-elected in 1692 and held office until 1694. He was also appointed president of the parliamentary visitation of Scottish universities to remove 'all such as continued attached to the house of Stuart.'[5] Other positions of importance held by Sir John were Member of Parliament, member of the Council to Advance Trade and Manufacture, Commissioner for Plantation of Kirks and Valuation of Teinds, and Commissioner of Militia and of Supply.[6] All the lands within the new Dunglass estate were ratified to Sir John Hall by an Act of Parliament on 17 July 1695, with a 'novodamus' erecting the whole into a free burgh of barony.[7] Sir John Hall died on 13 October 1695 and was buried in Greyfriars churchyard, Edinburgh. His son James succeeded to Dunglass and was served heir to his father on 30 November of that year.[8]

Sir James Hall, second baronet of Dunglass, was born in 1673[9] and as a young man it appears that he dealt with the business of the estate before his father died.[10] Like his father, Sir James married twice: first to Lady Anne Home, a daughter of Patrick, Earl of Marchmont, and secondly to Margaret, daughter of Sir John Pringle, baronet of Stitchell. James and Margaret had at least two sons named John, one born in 1706 and the other in 1711.[11]

Sir James' attitude to estate management in the early years of his stewardship suggests a remarkable inexperience, even by contemporary standards, and had little respect for religion.[12] He desecrated the old collegiate church of Dunglass by converting it into a stable, coach house, pigeon house and granary. In 1711 the English tourist who observed this wanton vandalism recorded that Sir James 'had gathered off all the gravestones of the churchyard to give scope for the growing of grass.' In making the nave of the church a stable Sir James had also 'dug up the graves of the dead, throwing away the bones to make way for a pavement for his horses.'[13] However, maturity seems to have somewhat educated this laird, for later on we find him planting trees in several parts of the parish. Long afterwards, in 1793, the seventy three year old Grizel Edington was living at Birnieknowes. As a girl she had watched the young plantations of Bilsdean, and it seems that Sir James had promised her a free house built from the wood when it was sufficiently grown.[14]

The coast between Fast Castle and Dunglass has over the centuries had its share of seafaring mishaps and tragedy. One such incident occurred in 1730, when a fishing boat got into difficulties. The fishermen, apparently from Dunbar, had been blown off course to the Isle of May. Next morning the tide brought them near Fast Castle, and the men seem to have been exhausted by their struggles. When news of their plight reached Sir James, he sent out a rescue boat with his bailie to refresh the men with bread, brandy and ale, so that on this occasion men and boat were luckily saved. The refreshments must have revived the fishermen's strength, for they went out again that night and caught more herring than any other boat from Dunbar except one.[15]

On 12 February 1733 Sir James Hall, for reasons which are not known, resigned Fast Castle and its farms to John Hall, his eldest son and heir. The lengthy legal document describes the battered remnants of the old stronghold as 'the Castle Tower Fortalice and Mannor place of Fast castle', giving no indication that it was either uninhabited or a ruin.[16] The document's main significance is its record that the farms of 'Wester Lumsden, Dowhill, Cauldside, Auldtown, Newton' and the castle were possessed and tenanted by 'John Boig', or Bogue, the first reference we have to a tenant of these lands as a complete unit. Sir James Hall died nine years later on 27 March 1742, as the result of 'a pluralic fever', which cannot have been helped by the two and a half hours' bleeding to which he was subjected.[17] Dunglass estate then passed to Sir John Hall, the third baronet, who was served heir to his father on 8 July 1743.[18]

The old barony of Dowlaw covered more or less the area represented by the modern Dowlaw Farm, which extends over approximately 1,000 acres. Together with the adjacent Redheugh Farm, both properties occupy some three square miles of the Berwickshire coast. 'Dula', as it is also known locally, now owned by Mr. Tom Dykes, is bounded on the east by Dowlaw Dean, on the south and west by Coldingham Moor, and the farms of Old Cambus and Redheugh [Plate 6]. Anciently forming part of the lands of Lumsden, Dowlaw presumably assisted in supplying Fast Castle with provisions, and may have been considered by the castle occupants as the 'home farm'. Until the eighteenth century, however, references to Dowlaw are mainly to be found in the Fast Castle charters and similar legal documents, which give little indication of agricultural practice. Then from the 1740s the details of local farming life are illustrated for the first time through the records of estate business accumulated by the Hall family.[19]

When Sir John Hall purchased Dunglass in 1687, Dowlaw and the other lands of Fast Castle would have looked very different from their appearance today. Now the single farm is made up of fields divided by about eight miles of dry stone dykes. These follow a rotation of corn, grass, and turnips, and support as many as 1,600 sheep in summer. There are also some eighty cattle, comprising thirty five breeding cows, thirty five calves, one bull and ten to fifteen young cattle. However, during the seventeenth and eighteenth centuries there was not one farm but several within the baronies of Fast Castle and Dowlaw. From the old charters already described, we know of the farms named Wester Lumsden, Dowlaw, Cauldside, Oldtown, and Newtown. The Dunglass estate ledgers provide us with a list of several others, including Eastfield, Large Muir, Cairnshot, Castleshot, Kingshill, Abbotlaw, Kirkbank, Farhill, Blackside, and possibly Fast Castle [Appendix 2 (c)]. In 1771 the barony of Dowlaw was measured at a scale of four English chains to the inch, and the completed survey included several of these farms together with their acreage. At that date the farm of Cauldside, for example, extended to 138 acres, its crop rental in 1761 being assessed at £33 2s 0d. In contrast, the farm of Abbotlaw covered an area of 33 acres, having a crop rental of £7 10s 7d.

The eighteenth-century records suggest that the crops being grown on most of these farms at that time were peas, corn, and wheat, although it is likely that 'bere' (barley) and oats were also harvested. As the accounts make only slight references to livestock, which included cattle, pigs and sheep, their numbers on each farm at any one time cannot be estimated. At the start of this period the land was farmed under the system of runrig or infield and outfield. Instead of a single compact holding, each farmer worked several strips, separated from each other and scattered about the infield or croft land, where most of the crops were grown year after year without a break. This continually cultivated land had to be well fertilised with animal manure, lime, or seaweed. Beyond lay the lands of the outfield which, due to their generally inferior quality, were used in a quite different manner. Here the sheep and cattle would graze and, depending on the particular situation, the farmer might be able to plough up parts of it for regular crop rotation where the land had been manured by controlled grazing. The outfield also produced building materials and turf for fuel. There were, of course, many variations within this general pattern, depending on the type of land under cultivation and the needs and capabilities of the individual farmer.[20] In a letter from John Wauchope, tenant at Redheugh, to Sir John Hall in 1764 there are signs that the use of the infield and outfield varied considerably from tenant to tenant [Appendix 2 (b)]. These arrangements survived in much of Scotland until the mid-nineteenth century. Exactly when the farms in the Dowlaw area changed over completely to the modern field layout is not clear, but parts of the old system were in operation as late as 1771.[21]

Although we cannot be sure to what extent the Dowlaw farmhouses of the eighteenth century fell into the normal Berwickshire pattern, some idea of their style may probably be gathered from a report on local agriculture published in 1809.

> Formerly the farm houses of this county were almost universally cottages, built of rough stone and clay mortar, and covered by thatch or sod. Some such still remain, even upon extensive arable farms, or old unexpired leases. The best of these contained only three small low roofed apartments, one of them the kitchen, all three with clay floors and bare walls, merely whitewashed, never ceiled, and seldom lofted. Now on every farm of any size the farm house is built substantially of stone

and lime, and consists of two stories, either slated or tiled, neatly
finished with lath and plaster, and every way fitted for the
comfortable and convenient accommodation of their respectable
inhabitants. The kitchen and household offices are neatly paved
with flat stones, and all the rooms boarded and ceiled. Many of
them are now greatly superior to the houses that were occupied
by the middling gentry 40 or 50 years ago. Anciently the
wretched farmers' cottages formed part of a miserable square or
row of offices, and opened immediately upon the dung hill or
muck court.

The author also describes the Berwickshire farmers as being

generally most respectable and intelligent, and their success has
been deservedly proportional. They have almost universally risen
completely above the class of peasantry, in knowledge,
education, and manners, assimilating in every respect to the
character of the country gentlemen. In every corner of the
country they are to be seen carrying on extensive and costly
improvements, by draining, inclosing, liming, and marling, and by
careful and judicious improvements of their livestock, sheep,
cattle, and even horses, with all the eagerness and intelligence of
commercial speculations, trusting to the certain profits of future
years to reimburse their large expenditures with reasonable
profit, which they are enabled to do through the sufficiency of
their capitals, and the security of their leases.[22]

But, as will be seen, the two tenant farmers who pioneered the new farming
methods at Dowlaw, failed miserably to match certain aspects of this
description.

Between 1755 and 1801 the population of Coldingham parish seems to
have remained static, varying only from 2,313 to 2,391 inhabitants. Numbered
among these in 1755 were the Bogues of Dowlaw, a family whose connection
with the farm appears to begin about 1700. John Bogue senior, portioner of
Auchencraw, was born in 1675 and became a tenant in Oldtown of Dowlaw
along with his father-in-law, David Crooks. Having married Agnes Crooks in
1697, John was made an elder in Coldingham Church prior to 1701. He
engaged in many land transactions, and in 1714 passed on the family property
of Auchencraw to his cousin, William Boig. John and Agnes had at least fifteen
children, including their son John, both father and son becoming joint tenants
of Dowlaw.[23]

In 1744, one year after succeeding as third baronet of Dunglass, Sir John
Hall had difficulties with his tenants at Dowlaw. A gross error was found in the
Bogue's accounts, whereby Sir John lost to the tune of £85 16s. The matter
was resolved by payments of cash or bills and wheat, and the Bogues were
discharged for the rent due on the lands of 'Fast castle' in 1741. During the

PLATE 10. Sir James Hall, 1761–1832. Eminent geologist, and President of the Royal Society of Edinburgh.

remainder of the Bogue tenancy, the rental for Dowlaw was £87 10s per annum, payable in the usual way at the two terms of Candlemas and Lammas. John Bogue senior died in 1749, and the management of Dowlaw was left to his son and family. John Bogue junior had married his cousin, Margaret Swanston, in 1739, and by the time they left Dowlaw in 1758 they appear to have had eleven children.[24] The family then moved to Hallydown Farm near Eyemouth, which John seems to have farmed until his death in 1786, and the Bogue family tombstone is still to be seen in Coldingham Priory churchyard. From 1758 to 1784 information on the tenants at Dowlaw is very sparse, and only two of their names are known: William Wight, who died in 1770 aged 54, and James Lounes, who apparently was in possession after him.

It was normal practice for a tenant farmer to lease his land for a term of nineteen or twenty one years, but during the Bogue, Wight and Lounes period longer leases were often granted as spurs to industry. Between 1770 and 1812 Dowlaw had at least three tenants, all of whom failed to complete their normal leases as a result of financial difficulties, caused partly by increasing rents and partly by the course of agricultural innovation. One result from this progress was the joining together of many of the smaller and less viable farms. In 1778 Cauldside and Windylaws were united, while in the same year Blackside and Farhill were amalgamated with Dowlaw.

Some of the initial improvement took place under Sir John Hall's control, but it was his son, Sir James Hall, the fourth baronet [Plate 10], who would actively promote the final transformation of the land into nearly its modern state. Sir James inherited Dunglass as a young boy of fifteen on his father's death in July 1776. Until his twelfth year he had been given a private education, but was then sent to a public school near London where he came under the care of his uncle, Sir John Pringle, the king's physician. About the time he inherited Dunglass, Sir James entered Christ's College, Cambridge. Later he made two European tours, acquiring valuable information on his special interests of geology, chemistry and Gothic architecture. In 1786, shortly after his return to Scotland, Sir James married Lady Helen Douglas, second daughter of Dunbar, Earl of Selkirk.[25] We have not yet established whether Sir James Hall spent any time at Dunglass between 1776 and 1786, but it is evident that for much of this period the property was under the direct management of someone else, possibly the estate factor.

One of the estate's most impressive sights, which must surely have gratified the returning Sir James, was the newly-built Pease Bridge, just outside Cockburnspath village on the road to Coldingham. Formerly all traffic going north or south had to cross over the ford at Pease Bay; the steep-sided glen spanned by the new bridge had previously been impassable, except to hardy souls of an adventurous spirit. The four-arched structure is some 300 feet long, 16 feet wide, and 127 feet high.[26] Although the bridge carried the London-Edinburgh traffic for another fifteen years, its importance was dramatically reduced by the completion about 1801 of the new post road via Grantshouse.[27] To appreciate the bridge's considerable height, it is necessary to stop and look over the parapet.

Sir James Hall was to become eminent in the field of geology and an intimate of James Hutton, the first scientist to show that the geological history of the earth could be interpreted in terms of processes continuing to the present day. Another close friend was John Playfair, the noted geologist and mathematician, from whom Sir James received a course in mathematics at a cost of £52 10s.[28] Sir James' interest in geology perhaps stemmed from his boyhood knowledge of the coastline between Dunglass and St. Abbs, for the rugged and majestic cliffs of Silurian greywacke and Old Devonian red sandstone have been described as one of the wildest cliff lines on Scotland's east coast. The contorted Silurian strata, in which Sir James Hall observed at least sixteen bends over a distance of five or six miles, have at some places, such as Fast Castle, been forced completely into the perpendicular.[29] There can be little doubt that the Dunglass geologist and his associates found much to inspire them in their studies of these remarkable phenomena. Sir James was also for some time president of the Royal Society of Edinburgh, and between 1808 and 1812 he represented the borough of St. Michael's in Cornwall as a Member of Parliament. In 1813, as a result of his architectural interests, Sir James published his once-celebrated *Origin, Principles, and History of Gothic Architecture*. Only five of his many children survived him, including the distinguished and much-travelled Captain Basil Hall.[30] Under the influence and efforts of Sir James and Lady Helen Hall, Dunglass estate was improved beyond recognition. Cockburnspath, judiciously managed by Lady Helen, lost its decayed and miserable appearance to become a neat, clean village.[31]

Much of Sir James' information on agricultural improvement apparently came from a visit he made in 1792 to Squire Eccleston, a noted Lancashire farmer. After careful observation of various aspects of 'modern' farming methods, Sir James wrote: 'I met with no single man from whom I learned so much in so short a time, and I felt I had still much more to get from him.'[32] Clearly this new knowledge was going to permanently alter the lives of many of Dunglass estate's inhabitants and, as the pace of improvement in farming techniques gathered speed, the disappearance of the old system became inevitable. Smaller farms were joined into larger units, forcing their tenants to take other employment on the estate, or move out of the area altogether. Such innovations, promoted by Sir James Hall and his father, required a new type of tenant, capable of adapting to the contemporary revolution in agriculture. These pioneers of the new methods would ideally be men with intelligence, skill and tenacity. Inevitably there were teething troubles with the developing technology; land was being ploughed up that had lain under grass from time immemorial, and it took much hard experience for the farmers to learn its characteristics, the particular sequence of crops, and quantities of fertiliser that would produce the best results in each field. Perhaps also farming at Dowlaw was made more difficult by the loss of grazing and other rights when Coldingham Common was divided in 1776.[33]

The first of the new tenants to lease Dowlaw was George Gilroy, who commenced his term in 1785, paying a rent of £250. This was raised to £425 in 1786 and £450 in 1788. Between 1787 and 1791 the accounts for Dowlaw suggest that a programme of building modernisation was under way, with much of the construction work carried out by Peter Hog, probably the local mason. During the first two years of this period Hog received £162 15s 3d, but regrettably his work is not itemised, except for 26s paid to him for erecting the barnyard dyke. Although Gilroy apparently made a serious attempt at farming Dowlaw, the high rent at least seems to have been a considerable problem. On 24 May 1792, after he had refused to find security for his arrears of £529 1s 7d, his crop and stock were sequestrated and sold by roup or auction. Gilroy left Dowlaw at the May term, but in April 1793 he still owed the same amount; while acknowledging the debt, he refused to sign the articles in the account. The matter was taken before the sheriff and the balance confirmed, although Gilroy did not appear in the case. William Reid, the next tenant at Dowlaw for whom we have a record, took over in 1795, this time for an annual rent of £525. At first Reid seems to have been more successful than Gilroy, for he survived on the farm until 1812. Eventually, however, Reid suffered the same fate as his predecessor, accumulating arrears of £1,473 19s 10½d. This must have seemed a poor reward for all his hard work, and a note in the account ledger comments that 'Mr. Reid's affairs got into confusion and he himself went mad.'

Despite Sir James's problems in obtaining his rent for Dowlaw, the Halls' annual disposable income rose from £2,300 in 1786 to £4,500 in 1806.[34] This increased prosperity led to the building of a new house at Dunglass, the foundation stone being laid down on 24 April 1807. Construction work on the house and associated farm buildings was not completed till February 1813, most of the stone being carted from quarries at Cove, a short distance away. The account book relating to the expense of erecting the new house shows that the final cost amounted to a little over £32,000. By comparison, in 1825 Sir James paid the princely sum of £98 for the erection of four farm servants' cottages on the farm of Redheugh.

William Reid's successor at Dowlaw was Francis Fairbairn, who entered his nineteen-year lease in 1813 for an annual rent of £600, representing an increase of a third over the rent paid by George Gilroy in 1788. Fairbairn seems to have been a farmer of a type very different from his predecessors Gilroy and Reid. Although he must have benefited from their pioneering efforts, he also managed the farm much more efficiently, only occasionally accumulating rent arrears. In 1828 Sir James Hall reduced the rent for Dowlaw to £500, his son Sir John Hall making a further reduction to £470 on the renwal of the lease in 1831. Fairbairn stayed on at Dowlaw until 1839 at least, when he disappears from the records. Robert Cowe, and later his sons Peter and William, continued the tenancy of Dowlaw. By 1879 the Edingtons occupied the farm, followed shortly after by the Purves family. Towards the end of the nineteenth century Norman Durie took over, and in 1919 he was succeeded by the Dykes family, who have held Dowlaw to the present time.

Sir John Hall, the fifth baronet, inherited the lands of Dunglass when his father died at Edinburgh on 23 June 1832.[35] Nine years earlier he had married Julia Walker, a daughter of James Walker of Dalry, and for at least part of their married life they appear to have had a second home in London. It was there that Sir John died on 2 April 1860, as did his wife in 1874. Over the next sixty years the estate passed through the hands of a further four members of the Hall family, before changing ownership. Dunglass finally passed from the Halls in 1919, when Sir John Richard Hall, the ninth baronet, sold the lands to Mr. Frank James Usher, whose family has owned the estate ever since.[36] Although it is nearly seventy years since the Halls owned Dunglass, the title in 1985 was still held by Sir Douglas Basil Hall, the fourteenth baronet.[37] In 1979 Dowlaw farm and the site of Fast Castle were purchased from Mr. Frank Usher by Mr. Tom Dykes.

Chapter 5

Fast Castle as an Antiquity

Fast Castle has probably had a longer career as a ruin, attracting the curiosity of visitors, than as an occupied residence. The first known reference to the castle being derelict appears in 1703, when it was described as 'Fals Castle, an old ruinous House, on the Point of a Rocky Promontory.'[1] The circumstances under which the castle was slighted and abandoned to the elements are, like its origins, shrouded in mystery. The initial destruction must have occurred at some date between 1651-2 and 1703, but most likely by the time that Sir John Hall acquired the property in the 1680s. As for the way in which this had happened, several possibilities must be considered.

The surviving remains of the entrance complex and keep may give the impression that the castle had suffered a very heavy bombardment by cannon [Plate 18]. However, this is improbable, for Fast appears to have surrendered to Cromwell's troops without a struggle. Some of the foundations, and in particular the curtain wall with adjoining rooms, seem to have been systematically levelled. The *History of the Berwickshire Naturalists' Club* for 1897 states that 'Fastcastle was one of the border fortresses which was dismantled under the provisions of an Act of Parliament.'[2] This explanation is entirely plausible, but no supporting evidence has been found in the Scottish Acts of Parliament. Another suggestion is that, having lain unused for many years, becoming more and more dilapidated, the castle was robbed for dyke building. That stone robbing did occur could until recently be seen in the crumbling remains of a dry-stone dyke at the bottom of Telegraph Hill. As late as the 1970s a dressed sandstone block from the castle was visible where the path to the castle crosses the old dyke. Over the centuries, the castle walls have also been eroded by wind and rain, and damaged by lightning. Lastly, it seems likely that the amusement of throwing stones from the walls into the sea some 100-150 feet below has denuded some of the castle's structure.

Although the fragmentary ruins of Fast Castle that survive at the present time are sufficient to confirm the relative accuracy of the 1549 plan, drawn for Henry, Earl of Rutland [Plate 19], many questions concerning the castle's original appearance still remain to be answered. By a close examination of the numerous illustrations of the castle, mainly produced during the nineteenth century, we have been able to establish certain basic facts about its construction.

The first of these pictures was published by Adam Mansfeldt de Cardonnel in 1793, in his *Picturesque Antiquities of Scotland.* Having been educated for the medical profession, Cardonnel initially practised as a surgeon, but his circumstances enabled him to spend a great deal of time on antiquarian pursuits. He was elected a fellow of the newly-formed Society of Antiquaries of Scotland in 1780, and from 1782 to 1784 served as its curator. Cardonnel became acquainted with Captain Francis Grose, the well-known English antiquary, and both men took part in various archaeological expeditions.[3] His

PLATE 11. Fast Castle: ruins of the keep or hall from the north, 1789.

PLATE 12. Fast Castle from the seaward (north), c. 1828. One of the more accurate of the early 19th-century illustrations.

PLATE 13. Fast Castle from the landward, c. 1822.

engraving of Fast Castle, made in 1789, shows the ruins of the hall, and the hall, and the outer wall of the brewhouse, as viewed from the north [Plate 11]. The position of the entrance to the hall is consistent with the 1549 plan, although the red sandstone dressings which would have embellished the door jamb appear to have been stripped out. The vertical breaks represented in the north wall occur roughly between where a probable window was situated, and the entrance into the area which has been designated the kitchen. The lump of masonry to the right of the hall may correspond to the mass which exists in a similar position today. Cardonnel's engraving is one of the more accurate illustrations of the castle, and it is unfortunate that he did not make other views of the site.

The individuals mainly responsible for popularising Fast Castle during the nineteenth century were Sir Walter Scott and his friend the Reverend John Thomson of Duddingston. In 1819, under the pseudonym of Jedediah Cleishbotham, Scott published *The Bride of Lammermoor*, which he had dictated during bouts of acute physical pain. The principal characters in this tragic novel are the Master of Ravenswood, who by the death of his father had inherited Wolf's Crag, and Lucy Ashton, to whom he became secretly betrothed. Lucy's mother, Lady Ashton, learning of the affair, set about separating the couple and, after Ravenswood left the country on a foreign mission, Lucy agreed to marry the Laird of Bucklaw. Immediately after the ceremony, Ravenswood challenged Lucy's brother and husband to fight duels on the following day. The same night, Lucy stabbed her husband, but died herself shortly after, while Ravenswood, galloping along the shore to meet his antagonists, was swallowed up by quicksand.[4]

Walter Scott based the story around historical events in the seventeenth century connected with Janet Dalrymple (daughter of the first Lord Stair), Lord Rutherford (to whom she was secretly engaged), and her husband David Baldoon. Subsequently considerable dispute has arisen as to whether Fast Castle was meant to represent the site of Wolf's Crag. Dunglass House and Cockburnspath Tower have each been claimed as the location, but Fast Castle, similar to the general description of the crag, seems more likely. While admitting that he had only seen Fast Castle from the sea, Sir Walter wrote that 'fortalices of this description are found occupying, like ospreys' nests, projecting rocks, or promontories, in many parts of the eastern coast of Scotland.' He continued rather enigmatically: '...the position of Fast Castle seems certainly to resemble that of Wolf's Crag as much as any other, while its vicinity to the mountain ridge of Lammermoor renders the assimilation a probable one.'[5]

Scott was educated at Edinburgh High School and later went on to the university, where he studied for a legal career. In 1792, at the age of twenty one, he was called to the Bar as a member of the Faculty of Advocates, and it was about this time that Scott and some of his colleagues would gather of an evening, for study and relaxation, in a house near Bristo Street. The lodging was occupied by the Thomson brothers, Adam, John, and Thomas, who came from Dailly in Ayrshire.

John Thomson, born in 1778 the youngest of seven children, showed an early and astonishing aptitude for his hobby of painting. Before and after school, and while on holiday, he was busily occupied with brush and pencil. Frequently he would rise at two in the morning, and tramp many miles, just to observe the sunrise from a particular spot. John longed to take up the life of an artist, but was finally forced to bow to the will of his father, the minister of the church at Dailly, that he too should become a minister. In 1791 John began his divinity course at the University of Glasgow but, after a session there, he came to Edinburgh University, following his brother Thomas who, like Walter Scott, was reading law. On the death of his father, John Thomson was ordained into his home church of Dailly in 1800. Although with little formal training, he continued to paint many scenes in his native Ayrshire. In 1805, thanks largely to the efforts of Walter Scott and his brother Thomas Scott, W.S., Thomson was translated to the much sought-after charge of Duddingston Church near Edinburgh. The move to Duddingston brought John into contact with many of the notable men of the time, and gave him much wider scope for his activities as a painter. It was here that Thomson's treatment of landscapes gradually blossomed into a romantic style, under the considerable influence of Sir Walter Scott. The two men became close friends and Scott was a frequent visitor to the manse, where a large part of *The Heart of Midlothian* was written.[6]

From 1822 to 1824 John Thomson apparently concentrated much of his efforts on painting the coastal scenery of Haddingtonshire and Berwickshire. During this period, he completed several views of Fast Castle, treating them, with one exception, in a highly romantic style. Although over the years the painter visited many parts of Scotland seeking subjects for his canvas, he seems to have become almost obsessed by Fast Castle. In 1919 Thomson's biographer, Robert Napier, listed some twenty known paintings of the castle by the artist, with information on their ownership, and in a number of instances their exhibition and publication. Perhaps John Thomson's most realistic view of the ruined fortress is the one he painted, about 1822, for his friend Sir Walter Scott [Plate 13]. Writing from Abbotsford on 9 January 1823 to Daniel Terry, son-in-law of Alexander Nasmyth, the novelist reported that 'John Thomson, Duddingstone, has given me his most splendid picture, painted, he says, on purpose for me – a true Scottish scene.'

The painting particularly pleased Sir Walter, as his description of it in the same letter shows:

> Now this is Fast Castle, famous both in history and legend, situated near St. Abb's Head, which you most certainly must have seen, as you have cruized along the coast of Berwickshire. The view looks from the land down on the ragged ruins, a black sky and a foaming ocean beyond them. There is more imagination in the picture than in any I have seen of a long time – a sort of Salvator Rosa's doings.[7]

The painting is briefly mentioned by William Douglas in his 1921 essay on the castle, where he suggested that it was 'doubtful if so much of the walls was standing then as is shown in this picture.' From a close examination of the painting, however, it seems likely that Douglas was mistaken. Allowing for artistic licence, the surviving remains of the hall are similar to Cardonnel's engraving of 1789, except that the view is from the other side. Perhaps Douglas's comment was based on the apertures depicted in the curtain wall. These may give the impression of windows, thus creating the effect of higher walls. During the summer of 1976 it was proved, with the aid of

PLATE 14. Tower of Wolf's Crag. Fast Castle was used as a model for illustrating various editions of Sir Walter Scott's *The Bride of Lammermoor.*

PLATE 15. View of Fast Castle from the seaward. A fanciful reconstruction based on Skene's illustration of 1828.

PLATE 16. Aumbry (or cupboard), showing remains of ogee arch, in east wall of hall or keep, 1961.

mountaineering equipment, that at least one of these openings is nothing more than a drain outlet.

In 1822 Joseph Turner, the celebrated English landscape painter, visited the manse at Duddingston. Both he and John Thomson had been chosen to provide illustrations for the planned publication of *The Provincial Antiquities of Scotland*, while Sir Walter Scott was employed to write the text. Finally published in 1826, this important work contained an equal number of plates from the paintings by Thomson and Turner, although Sir Walter would have preferred all the illustrations to have been by his old friend. Scott's highly coloured account of Fast Castle gives some idea of how he was able to weave words into a romantic image:

> These remarkable ruins are the remains of a gloomy border fortress, situated near to St. Abb's Head, on the iron-girdled shores of the German Ocean. Imagination can scarce form a scene more striking, yet more appalling, than this rugged and ruinous stronghold, situated on an abrupt and inaccessible precipice, overhanging the raging ocean, and tenanted of yore by men stormy and gloomy as the tempests they looked down upon. Viewed from the sea, Fast Castle is more like the nest of a gigantic roe or condor, than a dwelling for human beings, being so completely allied in colour and rugged appearance with the huge cliffs amongst which it seems jammed, that it is difficult to discover what is rock and what is building. To the land side, the only access is by a rocky path of a very few feet wide, bordered on either hand by a tremendous precipice. This leads to the castle, a donjon tower of moderate size, surrounded by flanking walls, as usual, which, rising without interval and abruptly from the verge of the precipice, must in ancient times have rendered the place nearly impregnable.[8]

The illustration by Thomson which accompanied this description shows what appears to be an unruined keep, perching insignificantly on top of a rugged headland. The lower half of the castle is completely omitted, the north face of the keep being situated on the sheer edge of the sea cliffs.

This theme was copied, more or less closely, by several artists during the next few years. One of the better illustrations of the castle is the engraving by James Skene in his *Localities of the Waverley Novels*, published in 1829 [Plate 12]. This is really an extension of Cardonnel's view, taken from the extreme end of the promontory. Apart from repositioning part of the curtain wall's surviving end-portion, it gives a good general idea of the site's appearance at this time. Over the following decades the castle was portrayed in a variety of publications although, regrettably, most of these illustrations are so fanciful that they provide little reliable information on architectural points. In some cases the degree of romanticism is so great as to make the castle almost unrecognisable. Melville's engraving of 1836, published in an edition of *The Bride of Lammermoor*, displays a complete two-storied keep with bartisans, set amongst a few other shattered remains [Plate 14]. Perhaps Clarkson Stanfield's view, made about 1851, is one of the better blends of realism and romance. Another engraving, which can only be described as a caricature of the castle, is found in Adam and Charles Black's *Picturesque Tourist of Scotland* of 1863 [Plate 15]. Apparently the artist had never visited the site, for his illustration is almost entirely fantastic. Having used James Skene's picture to reproduce the lower part of the castle, he superimposed a complete set of buildings on the upper level to give the appearance of an occupied residence. The scene is made quite ridiculous by two horsemen preparing to ride off the end of the promontory into the sea 100 feet below.

William Bartlett's engraving, published in 1859 for James Taylor's *Pictorial History of Scotland*, shows the upper level of the castle as viewed from the entrance causeway. This picture, although obviously inaccurate on some points, shows a structure that bears a striking resemblance to the ruins surviving now, except that the north wall of the keep as illustrated is more entire, with traces of a barrel vault, similar to that shown in Thomson's painting of 1822. In 1889 two rough sketches and a plan showing some of Fast's remaining fabric were published by the gifted illustrators of Scottish castles, the architects David MacGibbon and Thomas Ross.[9] These sketches, however, appear to have been drawn for them by Dr. James Hardy of Old Cambus, secretary of the Berwickshire Naturalists' Club. Depicted in one of the sketches is an inset drawing of a red sandstone aumbry or cupboard, situated in the north-east angle of the keep. Part of this aumbry remained as late as 1961, when it was photographed by the Royal Commission on Ancient Monuments (Scotland) [Plate 16], but now only some of its original outline can be seen.[10]

Despite exhaustive inquiries it has proved impossible to determine how many other illustrations of Fast Castle have been made over the years. Clearly several more exist, in particular those by minor and unrecorded artists. Turning to the present, it is worth remarking that the scene of historical desolation, set amidst the vastness of nature, still attracts the occasional landscape artist with his brush and easel.

The nineteenth-century visitor to Fast Castle must have found the task of getting there something of an expedition. Guides from Dowlaw were sometimes necessary, and the descent of Telegraph Hill perhaps held more dangers than at present. One visitor in 1829 advised that much care was required 'not to fall or slip in descending, as a false step might hurry the unwary traveller to the brow of a crag some hundred feet in height, and thence by one projection throw him into the boiling deep below.'[11]

As well as being visited by artists, the castle also drew the interest of antiquarians. Several excursions were made there by members of the Berwickshire Naturalists' Club on organised outings in the area. One attraction, current then and continuing to the present, is the study of the varied bird life that inhabits the tortured rock strata on the coastline between St. Abbs and Siccar Point. Nest-robbing was also practiced along this stretch of coast, as Robert Chambers recorded in 1827:

A number of stout young men, rather for amusement than for gain, employ themselves occasionally in scaling these dreadful and dizzy heights in order to steal the eggs of the birds. It would surprise a stranger to see with what confidence they perform their tasks, and to know that an accident does not occur among them, perhaps, once in a century. The secret seems to be, that a precipice which appears at a little distance quite sheer and plain, in reality presents many points to the gripe [sic] and step of the climber, and that what seems a narrow ledge, on which the foot could scarcely find room, becomes, when it is reached, a spacious platform. One man, many years ago, fell from a height of about four hundred feet, and left himself by instalments upon the rugged face of the rock. But that was owing to the faithlessness of a rope by which he had been let down; a mode of going to work which all true climbers hold in utter reprobation.[12]

Without doubt, the most impressive bird which used to inhabit the cliffs around Fast Castle was the peregrine falcon (Falco peregrinus). Apparently the species was breeding in the area as early as 1298 when two eyries, somewhere on this coastline, were recorded in a Coldingham rental.[13] Apart from this early reference, we have little or no other information on the peregrine prior to about 150 years ago. We can therefore only surmise that it had established its breeding pattern here, long before coming to the attention of ornithologists. Bone evidence from the excavations suggests that a member of the falcon family may on occasion have been eaten by the castle's inhabitants, and we must not overlook the possibility that they used the hawk for hunting purposes.

During the nineteenth century the noble bird was often sighted along the coast between St. Abbs and Fast Castle. It regularly made its nest in the vicinity of the castle, sometimes on the adjacent cliffs, aptly named Hawksheugh. Peter Cowe, while tenant of Dowlaw, reported that in June 1860 'he took four young Peregrines out of their nest in the precipice at Hawksheugh, immediately to the east of Fast Castle. He was drawn up the face of the cliff from the beach, by four or five men stationed at the top of the rock, with a long rope, a chain being attached to the upper part of the rope to come in contact with the rocks and thus prevent the danger of its chafing on their sharp points.'[14] The process seems to have been repeated in 1866 by Peter's brother, William. This daredevil practice must have required very considerable courage and strength, and shows to what lengths men will go to obtain something they prize. The eyrie at Fast Castle was occupied as late as 1920, when our information on the peregrine's further activities here ceases.

A large proportion of the castle's visitors are now birdwatchers, for whom the walk from Dowlaw must certainly be worth the effort. In early summer the north face of the promontory is completely covered by nesting gulls, a most spectacular sight. One ever-popular attraction is the annual visits by colourful puffins, while from time to time racing pigeons use the castle as a resting place.

In 1871 Fast Castle possibly suffered the last major assault on its walls, when the remains of the keep were said to have been almost demolished by a bolt of lightning. The effect on the castle's appearance may have been quite significant, especially to those who had known it over the years. In a letter written by James Hardy of Old Cambus in 1874, he describes the ruins as 'very fragmentary, having been struck by lightning, and the keep turned upside down, and only a wall of it left.'[15]

It was at this time that a young shepherd lad called Walter Chisholm could be found tramping the fields and braes in the area of Redheugh. About the age of twelve, Walter had to give up his education to help his father, who in 1865 became shepherd on this farm. While caring for his flock, Walter must have spent many an hour meditating on his surroundings for, by the early 1870s, neighbourhood gossip suggested that he was writing poetry. In 1875 the family moved to Dowlaw but, as he was not required at his new home, the young poet took on summer employment in the district of Yetholm. In the winter he resumed his schooling at Old Cambus and, on entering a poetry competition for the *People's Journal*, his poem entitled 'Scotia's Border Land' won second prize. Walter's poems on the locality, such as 'The Lines on St. Helen's Church', 'The Pease Glen', and 'Fast Castle', show remarkable inspiration and quality from one so young, particularly when his background is taken into account [Appendix 4]. In 1876 Chisholm went to Glasgow, where he was employed as a porter in a leather warehouse. Tragically, the budding poet's life was cut short, for, when visiting his parents at Dowlaw, he suffered a debilitating attack of pleurisy. Although he rallied, he never fully recovered and died at Dowlaw on the lst of October 1877.[16]

During the early part of this century, interest in Fast Castle took on a more investigative turn when William Douglas brought to light many previously unknown facts about its history. An amateur archaeologist and historian, Douglas was also for many years actively concerned with the Scottish Mountaineering Club. From 1892 to 1909 he was the club's Honorary Editor, and he contributed over fifty articles and notes to its *Journal.* Having found great joy roaming the hills of Scotland, Douglas's climbing career also extended over several other European countries as well as Canada.[17]

Not long before his article on the castle was published in 1921, Douglas produced a report on a survey undertaken in May 1920 of the huge sea cave which lies beneath it.[18] This first recorded examination of the cave seems to have taken place in an attempt to prove or disprove reports of a concealed staircase between the castle above and the roof of the cavern. When the nineteenth-century accounts of this hidden passage are considered, it is not surprising that Douglas felt the exercise worthwhile. They all stem from Alexander Carr's *History of Coldingham Priory*, published in 1836, which states: 'According to tradition, there was a communication between the castle and a large cavern at its base, by means of a stair constructed through its heart, which if it existed, must have contributed greatly to the security of the castle during a seige.'[19]

Along with the main cave, a second and smaller one is situated directly under the furthest point of the promontory. Access to both is difficult and would normally be made from the sea or with the benefit of mountaineering expertise. An alternative means of entrance to the main cave involves a detour over the top of Hawksheugh, followed by a scramble down a steep slope to sea level, and from there along the rough foreshore to the base of the promontory. This was the route attempted by Douglas on 22 May 1920. After reaching the base, however, he discovered that it was a matter of so near, yet so far: several yards of what must have been extremely cold sea-water barred his way. The following day he was joined by two of his mountaineering associates, Harold Raeburn and George Sang, who enthusiastically volunteered to swim the gap. While Douglas waited near the entrance, the other two explored the cave with a candle.[20]

> They estimated that it ran back about eighty yards, and terminated in a little tunnel with slimy bits of broken wreckage. There was every indication that the waves at high tide lashed right in to its very end. They found the walls of the cave were solid sheets of rock which gradually converged as they advanced. The floor was of slippery rock, covered near the entrance with a beautiful sea-lichen resembling a pink coral in colour, which changed, as they advanced, into an unspeakably slimy mud

well-nigh impossible to walk on. There was not the slightest appearance of an aperture in its roof, nor was there any trace of cut steps on its walls.

After this examination Douglas concluded that the alluring tradition had been discredited, and that it was necessary to abandon the idea of there ever having been a passage from the cave to the castle. He did not find this a pleasant conclusion, but felt that, as the castle was so rich in historical associations, it could afford to loose one and yet still remain a place of great interest.[21]

In May 1924 members of the Berwickshire Naturalists' Club visited the castle on one of their outings. A brief history was given by the Secretary, based on the articles by Douglas, who was also a member of this group. A few days before, three of the members had carried out two small archaeological probes at the castle. One was near the path adjacent to the brewhouse, where they uncovered six steps of red sandstone and found some roof slates, measuring about 18 by 12 inches. The second probe took place at the well, situated on the mainland not far from the castle entrance. The well head was cleared out and observed to have a surround of sandstone coping blocks.[22]

The first recorded air reconnaissance of Fast Castle appears to have been made by a Mr.Ian Campbell in 1933 although, by his own admission, the plan he produced afterwards was unconvincing. Continuing the efforts of Douglas, Raeburn, and Sang, Campbell and his brother explored both caves. Having reached the Cyclopean chamber by means of climbing and swimming round the end point of the promontory, the pervading atmosphere seems to have had an unnerving effect on the adventurous brothers. Campbell's account of their experience conveys some idea of what lies in store for the unwary visitor:

> As we neared the far end of the cave the light grew dim and the small circle of daylight at the cave mouth seemed terribly far away. The gurgle and rumble of the incoming waves was repeated hoarsely by the lichen-covered walls, and we peered anxiously into the gloom as if fearing to meet some Obscene Presence that might have its dwelling place in this unholy cavern. As I moved forward towards the blackness my foot slipped on something smooth and slimy wet. I did not have the sensation of falling, but some unseen force seemed to draw my limbs down and over the slippery rock until I found myself crawling and stumbling forward on all fours. Ultimately the end of the tunnel was reached, and it was with a sigh of relief that we turned and made our way hurriedly towards the sea and freedom.[23]

In 1935 H. Drummond Gauld, another member of the Society of Antiquaries, suggested that a skilful excavation of the site would reveal the plan of the vanished castle and bring to light much that remained obscure.[24] However, many years would pass before this idea was put into effect. From the later 1930s to 1968 investigation of the castle's many mysteries seems to have been at a low ebb, as little published information is available for the period. Nevertheless, it must be assumed that the panoramic view and the old ruin's other attractions continued to draw casual visitors, and those with more specific interests.

Then suddenly, in the summer of 1969, a flurry of activity engulfed the remnants of the old castle walls as Fred Douglas began his search for buried treasure. The castle was visited by Douglas's helpers on most weekends during the summer, and probes were made at several points. The search continued during the summer of 1970, with the digging now concentrated in the outer half of the lower courtyard. During this two-year period Douglas contacted several psychic diviners, who apparently thought that treasure of some kind was to be found in the castle's vicinity. The site was also visited by members of the Eyemouth Sub-Aqua Club and pot-holers from the Grampian Speleological Group. They explored the sea bed around the promontory and the large cave, finding a rock-cut basin near the cave entrance and a fissure in the cave wall. This rift was found to reach for some way, but apparently came to a dead end, except for a draught of air blowing from an unknown source.[25]

At this time Fast Castle and its reputed associations with hidden treasure were described in several newspapers, and on one occasion received brief coverage by Scottish Television. The probes made in the lower courtyard turned up a variety of finds, including animal bones, pot sherds, shells, and a few sixteenth-century coins, all items typical of a Scottish medieval castle. However, no evidence of a 'treasure' came to light and in 1971 work at the site was put on a less glamorous but more systematic basis, under the direction of the association which shortly afterwards became the Edinburgh Archaeological Field Society.

Chapter 6

Excavations at Fast Castle, 1971-86

When during the summer of 1971, in what seems an age ago, our Society first started wielding the trowel at Fast Castle, it was never envisaged that excavations would still be continuing some sixteen years later. As time passed, particularly after 1980, those who had lasted the pace from the beginning, and a number of later recruits, began to wonder when the work would be completed. Some 150 volunteers have taken part in this rather unusual venture, ranging in age from under ten to over seventy. Our ever-changing team of volunteers has trowelled, shovelled and riddled its way through tons of assorted soil, clay and ash levels, and hand picked mountains of muscle-binding rubble. Although much was accomplished with the help of those who visited the site only once or twice, the excavations could not have been completed without a dedicated core of enthusiasts. As work progressed the excavations were inspected by various specialists who gave technical advice, on soil analysis for example. While this kind of information was invaluable, members of our own group provided the necessary expertise in photography, surveying, and many other skills. Naturally our project attracted all types of people, including those of a mildly eccentric disposition, a tendency likely to be accentuated by the prolonged excavational saga. Probably I should include myself in this description.

The fact that Fast Castle lies some forty miles from Edinburgh limited the amount of work the excavators were able to accomplish on any one outing. On Sunday, our usual 'Fast' day, it was Society practice to congregate by 9.30 a.m. opposite the Royal Scottish Academy, Princes Street, as the point of departure for Berwickshire. This starting time put considerable strain on some of even the keenest diggers, myself included, who occasionally would have preferred extra time in bed. Early in the excavations we used to visit the castle almost every Sunday between April and September, but during the last few years this was reduced to a fortnightly excursion.

When peering bleary-eyed through the bedroom curtains, only to see fog with visibility at perhaps twenty yards, torrents of rain, or other inviting weather patterns, common sense obviously suggested that a return to the 'Land of Nod' was best for all concerned. However, knowing that the show must go on, our 'heroic squad' would soon be roaring down the A1 into East Lothian and Berwickshire. Yet the decision to go, whatever the weather in Edinburgh, was nearly always correct, cloud-laden skies or steady rain frequently giving way to bright sunshine in the neighbourhood of Cockburnspath, or even while descending the hill to the castle. On warm, sunny days Fast Castle is an idyllic spot at which to pass away the hours, although it undergoes a dramatic character change under the influence of wet or windy weather. New members and visitors who were making the journey to Fast Castle for the first time would often receive a potted history of sites of interest seen in the passing, such as Traprain Law and Cockburnspath Tower. Latterly we were able to point out, to those who had not seen it before, the weird new monolith that sits, so 'unobtrusively', at Torness Point.

Over the years one of the most frustrating aspects of our adventures was the simple exercise of getting to and from the castle, after leaving the cars at Dowlaw cottages. The three-quarter mile walk over and down Telegraph Hill is normally quite straightforward [Plate 17], but we had to take special care when lugging heavy or awkward equipment to and from the site, particularly after heavy rain. At this point a little story of a roll of wire netting may illustrate the dangers of trying to take short cuts. At the beginning of the season in 1976 this roll was being taken down to the castle, to refence the trenches under excavation. At the steepest point of the hill, in an attempt to save some energy, the roll was sent down by itself, the idea being that it should 'run freely into the fence at the bottom.' The plan disastrously backfired, with the roll making 'its own mid course correction half way down.' Louping the low dry stone dyke adjacent to the fence, 'it then proceeded at an ever increasing rate across the field eventually launching itself over the cliff edge' some 350 feet above the sea. 'Most mortals would have cried enough, not so three intrepid members of the Society who set about investigating the possibility of recovery.' Some two hours later, after much hard labour, the roll was brought back from the sea-shore. The following day, one of the retrievers was still apparently suffering from *rigor mortis.*[1]

For about two years another approach to the castle was followed, along what may have been part of the original road from Dowlaw, which today ends in the middle of a large field near the summit of Hawksheugh. This track certainly offered distinct advantages over Telegraph Hill, but in wet weather had its own unique problems. On one occasion in 1979 a carload became bogged down in the field below Dowlaw. It was a case of get out and push, with the inevitable comedy routine being performed. After the owner's wife had been installed behind the steering wheel, 'the "heavy squad" applied pressure to the rear end of the car. Unfortunately at this juncture the pilot appears to have been overcome by a sudden rush of blood to the right foot. This resulted not as was intended in the vehicle being propelled forward, but in the ground being propelled back to be deposited uniformly on the countenances of the heaving scrum at the rear, no doubt evoking a number of linguistic pearls.'[2]

Throughout the 1971 digging season, a major problem was the necessity of transporting all our equipment to and from the site on each day's work there. As may be imagined, this proved not only tiresome, but a disenchanting exercise for many of our volunteers. So it was agreed that the provision of a storage hut would make life much easier. In March 1972 a standard 6 by 4 feet garden hut was purchased, along with several sheets of corrugated iron to clad it for added protection. Sunday 24 March, when the structure was put up, turned out to be one of the most exhausting days I have experienced at Fast Castle. By 9 a.m. the sections and metal sheets had been loaded onto a trailer, and later in the morning they were deposited in the field above Hawksheugh. The sections were then laboriously manhandled across the field to the top of the hill overlooking the castle and carefully lowered, one by one, to their final resting place. Needless to say, there followed a well-earned break for refreshments, after which for several hours the normally peaceful scene turned into a hive of industry. It was not until the unprecedented departure time of 8 p.m. that Fast Castle had been given its first new construction in several hundred years.

PLATE 17. Fast Castle from Telegraph Hill, 1986.

PLATE 18. Fast Castle from the landward, 1986, showing: (left) remains of entrance with modern steps and chain-fenced causeway; (centre right) corner of keep or hall still surviving to the corbel table.

PLATE 19. Sketch plan of Fast Castle, based on a plan made in 1549 for the 2nd Earl of Rutland. The shaded areas indicate the present visible remains.

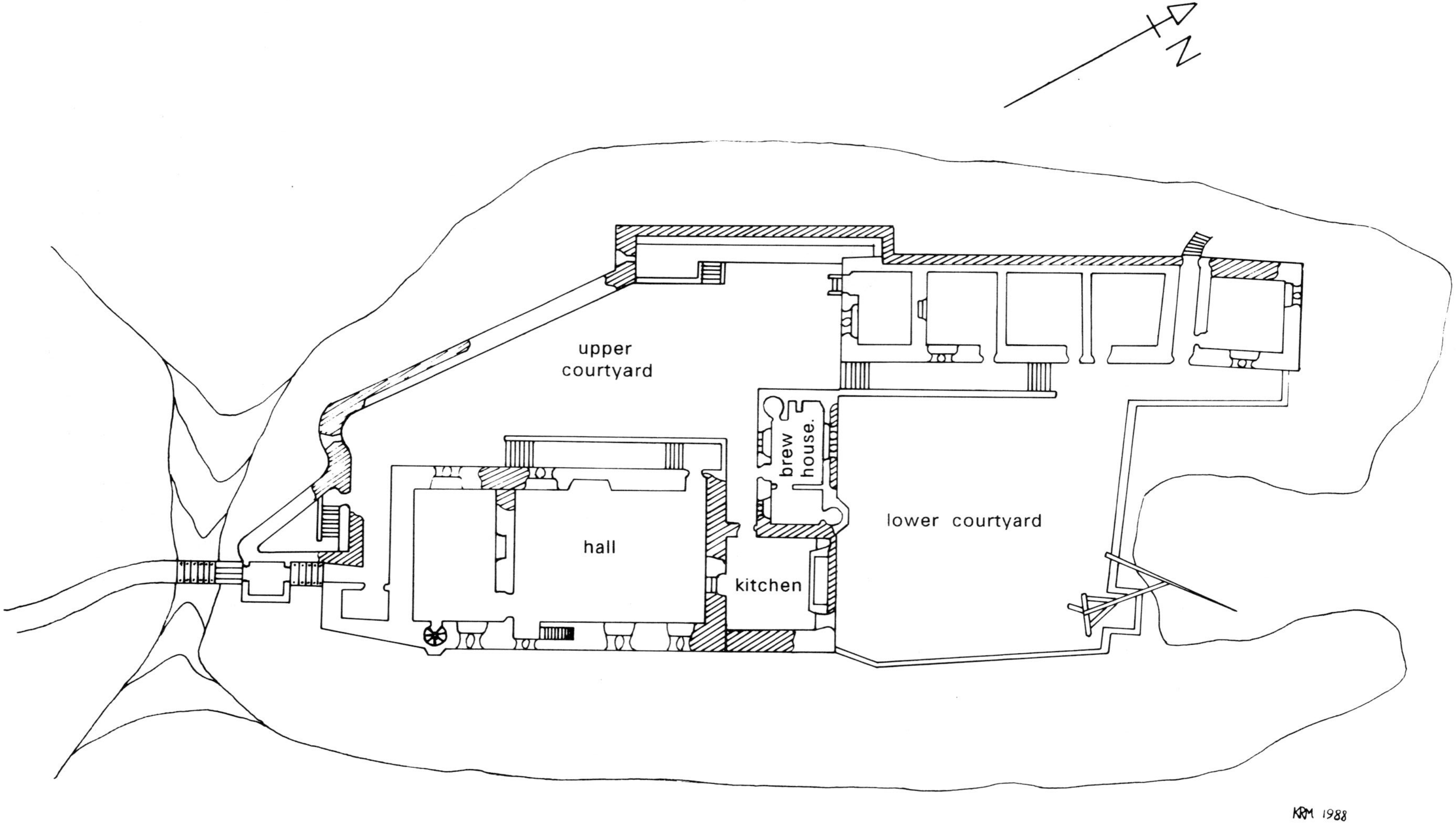

lower courtyard

brew house.

kitchen

upper courtyard

hall

K&M 1988

The hut proved to be a considerable asset throughout the subsequent excavations but, perhaps not surprisingly in these modern times, it has suffered several attacks from vandals. On one occasion we arrived at the site to find the hut leaning towards the sea at an angle of almost 45 degrees. The metal cover over the door had been prised off and the door itself flung over the cliffs. In order to repair the hut and protect the equipment, which luckily was almost untouched, I had to make a treacherous descent of the cliffs to reclaim the door. I must admit that, on returning to the horizontal plane, my thoughts respecting the perpetrators were less than pleasant.

With Fast Castle being in such an exposed position, and the elements varying from the sublime to the almost ridiculous, new recruits were always advised to dress accordingly. At the start and end of each season protection from rain or a biting cold wind was generally obtained by a large assortment of anoraks, cagoules and woolly jumpers. When genuine summer sunshine made a visit to the castle a particular pleasure, this type of clothing was abandoned for the more comfortable T-shirt. Stout walking shoes or trusty 'wellies', were essential to avoid blisters or sprained ankles, and hard-wearing gloves were very useful in helping to protect the hands from cuts and abrasions while working with the sharp-edged rubble. Although the majority of our members followed these fashion 'norms', there were some exceptions, most notably the late Mr. Gardiner (Big Gee), who always came to the castle in a three-piece suit and trilby. A much respected member of the Society, Gee could never be imagined in 'trendy digging gear'. Some of our group have from time to time taken the precaution of using safety helmets. On one occasion, while looking over the cliff face above the large cave, my helmet slipped off and was lost, I thought forever, in the sea below. To my surprise I learned that a few days later the helmet was recovered from Dunbar harbour, when some of our group were on a visit there.

Usually our team of excavators would be on site and ready for action a little after 11 a.m., although in 1986, during the process of backfilling, one extra-keen member was often to be found at the unearthly hour of 7.30 a.m. moving vast quantities of turf, soil and rubble. The day's first task was the 'ceremonial' opening of the hut, to get the necessary tools including trowels, brushes, buckets, riddles, ranging poles and barrows. To help protect our equipment, six sturdy bolts kept the metal cover over the wooden door and, when they had become rusted up, a curious pantomime would be enacted in an effort to release the nuts. However, such minor difficulties paled into insignificance when, from time to time, it was discovered that nobody had brought a spanner!

After the tools were carted into the castle, a quick conference would be held to decide on the day's activities, led by Eric Robertson, when he had sole charge of the excavations from 1973 to 1983. During this ten year period Eric was the driving force behind all the activities at the castle, and his output and commitment to the excavations were phenomenal. Lunchtime was normally about 1 p.m. and, on days when the weather took a turn for the worse, this occasion could prove a severe trial. There is something distinctly unappetising about soggy, loam-filled sandwiches, and attempts to drink soup or tea in a force 10 gale tend to leave half the beverage dripping down one's chest or legs. Excavations would then restart about half an hour later, except on sunbathing days, and continue until about 4.30 p.m. although, during the first few years, a finishing time of 6 p.m. was not unusual.

From the beginning, almost every day's work produced several bags of assorted finds, including pot sherds of mainly Scottish origin and the remains of countless medieval 'banquets'. To retrieve fragments of pottery was always considered important, but animal bones and oyster shells turned up in such abundance that congratulations were reserved for more exciting finds. Another significant aspect of the excavations was the discovery of wall foundations which had not seen the light of day for perhaps three or four hundred years. I must confess that to take part in uncovering these was personally a most rewarding experience. Certainly, establishing their existence has greatly enhanced our interpretation of the 1549 plan of the castle. After work for the day was completed and the tool hut resealed, workers in various stages of dishevelment would prepare for what some longstanding participants described as the worst part of each visit. This was the ascent of 'Mount Telegraph Hill', which a few of our younger and fitter members could run up in about ten minutes. Wiser methods were employed by those of us who preferred to transport our tired limbs and gasping lungs more sedately. With conversation more or less dropping to nods and grunts, people would be heard fantasising about chairlifts and heliports!

The need to ensure a degree of continuity with the treasure hunt, and to rescue archaeological information that otherwise might have been lost, meant that excavations began in the area which we designated the lower courtyard. Situated some 100 feet above the entrance to the main cave and measuring about 55 by 65 feet, the courtyard was divided roughly into two parts. The outer, northern half, bounded by the cliff face and the well-trodden visitors' path, had been completely grassed over prior to the treasure hunt. The inner half, inclined at both ends, was largely covered during the summer months by a mass of nettles.

Throughout the digging seasons of 1971 to 1974 we concentrated on excavating the outer part of the courtyard, and two small, partially-turfed areas in the inner half. No major problems occurred and most of these areas were excavated to bedrock or wall foundations. In the north-east corner of the outer courtyard a small area paved with flagstones lying a few inches above bedrock was uncovered. Nearby we also found the remains of a peculiar curved wall foundation. During the treasure hunt the upper surface of this wall had yielded part of an iron cannon. Then, in the north-west corner, the flattened remnants of a small room slowly began to emerge from centuries of interment. Unfortunately, the demolition had been almost complete, reducing the foundations to one or two courses of masonry, except for one possible connecting wall. Entry into the room had been gained by descending two small steps, beside which we were surprised to find a fragment of plaster still adhering to the bedrock.

Because the lower courtyard is depicted as featureless on the 1549 survey [Plate 19], apart from rampart walls and a schematically-drawn crane and bucket device, it seems safe to assume that all the structures located in the outer area predate this plan, a supposition apparently confirmed by several late fifteenth-century coins found in the lowest levels. It seems that the function of the whole courtyard dramatically altered about the middle of the sixteenth century, when it was levelled off with a thick deposit of soil, probably brought into the castle from the mainland.

The coins employed to date the lower levels are a series of the so-called 'Bishop Kennedy pennies', and one tiny Crossraguel farthing. The 'pennies' used to be considered quite rare. However, during the past few years specimens have turned up on many sites throughout Scotland. Recent investigations suggest that these coins, which previously had been classified as ecclesiastical issues of James Kennedy, Bishop of St. Andrews (c.1440-65), are more likely to come from the regal coinage of James III (1460-88). If this re-classification is correct, it implies that our 'pennies' were roughly contemporary with the early occupation of the castle by Sir Patrick Home during the 1480s. In the upper soil levels coins of Mary, Elizabeth, and James VI were found, together with possible forgers' blanks for Charles II turners. One of these levels also yielded a decorated pipe bowl of Dutch origin, dated to between 1640 and 1670, contemporary with the castle's last phase of occupation.[3]

Many other interesting items were recovered from their long burial, bringing to light some of the secrets of the old ruin and its inhabitants. Such finds included spindle whorls used for weaving, numerous musket balls, iron and lead cannon balls, copper buckles, and a first- or second-century A.D. dress fastener. The discovery of this last object was unexpected, but not quite so astonishing as it might at first seem. Similar fasteners have been found at the fortified Iron Age settlement of Traprain Law, at one time the capital of the British tribe known as the Votadini. Perhaps this specimen was lost by its owner when admiring the view near the promontory, before going back to his home in the contemporary settlement which has been identified near Dowlaw Farm. Also, as we shall see, there may be evidence for Iron Age occupation immediately adjacent to the Fast Castle promontory. The most vivid record of human activity among our discoveries was the smashing of a large earthenware vessel by a stone ball. Some of the sherds were left in situ, along with the offending ball, and one is left wondering if this was the outcome of a children's game, the work of a bored servant or soldier, or the result of a direct hit during an attack on the castle.

After completing excavation of the outer lower courtyard, we next turned our attention to the inner part, and it was while working on the upper levels of this area in 1976 that investigations began into other aspects of the castle and its promontory. First, a survey was undertaken of Fast Castle's two caves, a project which had proved quite beyond the capabilities of our Society. While contemplating the mouth of the main cave during moments of relaxation from the toil above, we often reflected on the tradition of a stairway between the cave and castle, and the problems of exploring the dark recesses below. But the likelihood of our doing so seemed remote until late in 1975 when, quite by chance, I had the good fortune to discuss the situation with Captain Richard Powell, RAOC, who was stationed in Edinburgh. With a view to organising an expedition for surveying the caves, he immediately contacted a friend, Lieutenant Adrian Ashby-Smith, RAOC, of St. George's Barracks, Bicester, who had been on expeditions organised by Lieutenant-Colonel Blashford-Snell.

In true army style, preliminary meetings were arranged in double-quick time to assess the feasibility of the proposed venture. The first meeting was held within the walls of Edinburgh Castle, which also gave me the opportunity of sampling the culinary delights of the officers' mess. The second came at Captain Powell's home, where I was introduced to Adrian, who had journeyed north to learn at first hand of the archaeologists' requirements and to familiarise himself with the site. As enthusiasm for the survey gained momentum, those of us most involved with Fast Castle began to hope that, before the year was out, we might solve the mystery of that elusive passage, and at the same time obtain valuable new information on both caves. Adrian appeared to be suitably impressed by his visit to the castle and, with only a few organisational matters to attend to, the expedition, cunningly code-named 'Jock Trap', was as good as off the ground.

After permission for the undertaking had been secured from Adrian's Commanding Officer, the eight members of the army team, made up of five RAOC and three WRAC personnel, put in many hours' training, described by one of Adrian's reports:

> The climb leader, L.Cpl. Alan Cotterill, continued his permanent spare time occupation of ascending and descending on any form of natural features worthy of his attention. Elementary ropework techniques, and acquaintance with numerous specialised items of equipment, occurred within the confines of St. George's Barracks. Thus it was that trees were festooned with ropes and ladders, and the Miniature Range became a depository for rations, generators, and a multitude of other assorted items – probably a source of great speculation to regular users of the range.[4]

On 6 June 1976 Adrian and his team, with the co-operation of Mr. Usher and Mr. Dykes, set up camp not far from the summit of Hawksheugh. During the next ten days the caves and cliffs resounded to the labours of the explorers, who were often forced to work in very uncomfortable conditions. Naturally, several Society members expressed a desire to enter the main cave and see at first hand the findings of the intrepid climbers. Adrian agreed to this, and so on Sunday 13 June a small army of part-time archaeologists arrived at the promontory, where they awaited L.Cpl. Alan Cotterill's commands, or peered over the edge at the antics of the volunteers.

Stout ropes encircled part of the curtain wall and dangled down to the side of the cave entrance. Robin Murdoch, the first 'brave' volunteer, prepared for the giddy abseil yet, as he walked backwards over the cliff edge, his second thoughts became obvious to all those watching [Plate 21]. Within a few seconds, however, he overcame the natural instinct to replace his feet on the horizontal, and soon afterwards he was standing at the base of the cliff. Following Robin's example, I too found myself teetering on the brink, and the first few hesitant steps, taken at a 75 degree angle, were perhaps the most frightening of my life. By the time I had descended about half-way, the enjoyment felt by the professional mountaineer had taken hold and, on reaching the bottom, I was craving to repeat the experience, no doubt a rather foolish notion, as I would discover later. My next initiative was unfortunate. Having decided to cross by a rope stretched over the channel in front of the cave, in order to photograph the promontory's base from the opposite side, I began a slow and clumsy traverse in an upside-down crawling position. About halfway over, due to either my weight or lack of technique, I felt my back suddenly dip into the freezing cold water. As a result my camera received a brief and unintended soaking, which ruined all further attempts at photography for the day.

When eight Society members were collected beside the entrance, Adrian and some of his team conducted us, wading and clambering over the uneven

PLATE 20. Fast Castle from the air, 1980. [See Plate 1.]

PLATE 21. Robin Murdoch abseiling to the cave entrance during the army excavation of the cave, June 1976.

PLATE 22. Excavation in the inner lower courtyard, 1985.

and slippery surface, to their work area some 260 feet away in the bowels of the ancient rock. With the aid of generator-powered lights we were able to examine the upper part of the extension to the cave, which Adrian's group had begun to reveal by the removal of flotsam and a sticky mixture of clay and rubble. Although observers might have been forgiven for thinking that symptoms of insanity were appearing in these atrocious conditions, enthusiasm was now at a high point amongst the mud-encrusted human moles. They were inspired by the belief that some form of communication between the cave and castle might yet be discovered.

All too soon, however, the time available for our exploration ran out, and we were escorted back along the dark passage to the glorious sunlight. Standing once more at the base of the cliff-face, the route upwards suddenly appeared much less inviting than our recent descent. Following instructions to shout 'climbing' or 'hold' as and when necessary, we slowly clawed our way up the almost vertical incline. For me the first few yards were fairly easy, but about halfway up I began to suffer painfully from the tremendous strain on my arms. The hoarse grunt of 'hold' came frequently from my lips; when I finally crawled panting over the top, my arms felt as if they were made of lead, and stretched to twice their normal length. The fact that we all arrived safely back at our starting point was largely due to the skill and stamina of Alan Cotterill, the hero of the hour.

After some discussion about Adrian's future plans, he presented the Society with a crest of the Sixteenth Battalion, a fine momento of the day's activities. His next climbing project was much further afield: he had arranged to take part that August in an international expedition studying geothermic energy on Ecuador's 17,160 feet high Sangay Volcano.[5] However, as the survey of the Fast Castle caves had proved both exciting and rewarding, Adrian hoped that on his return from Sangay the team would be able to continue investigations under the heading of 'Jock Trap 2'. Although farewells were exchanged by some on the following day, most of the group said their goodbyes on leaving the castle, as our army friends went back to work in the cave. So we then set off up Telegraph Hill, exhausted, but cheerfully talking over the day's experiences, unaware that a tragedy was soon to occur thousands of miles away, which would cost the life of a friend and stop exploration in the caves for the forseeable future.

One evening in mid-August, little more than two months later, radio news bulletins began to carry reports of a climbing accident in Ecuador, immediately making us anxious for Adrian's safety. It soon became clear that Sangay had suddenly erupted, with devastating consequences for the six-man British team which had been climbing near to its summit at the time. Two deaths were reported, along with injuries to the remainder of the team, and for the next few days we could only hope and pray that Adrian was among the survivors. But eventually our worst fears were confirmed by the terrible news that Adrian had indeed been killed, together with the expedition cameraman, Ronald Mace.

The British team had been approaching the rim of the crater, on 12 August, when the volcano erupted without warning, sounding 'like an artillery bombardment'. Describing the catastrophe, an Ecuadorian geologist, Senor Gerardo Herrera, said that the 'mountain shook and a huge red cloud erupted from its snow-covered peak'. Then stones, lava, and fire rained down, crackling like a bonfire.[6] The explosion hurled rocks on to the climbers, who were sent tumbling some 2,000 feet down the volcano. All were badly injured, except

Major Nick Cooke, the climb leader. Richard Snailham and cameraman Peter Chadwick went to get help and, shortly after they left, Major Cooke discovered that Ronald Mace had died from severe head wounds. Adrian, who was also suffering from serious head injuries, and the expedition leader, Captain Jan Iwandzuik, who was in a coma, were cared for as much as the adverse circumstances would allow by Major Cooke. He struggled through the rest of the day and a bitterly cold night to keep the two men alive. By 7 o'clock the following morning, as no rescue had been effected, Major Cooke decided to leave his colleagues to seek help, and laboriously made his way to base camp. Later that day an exhausted group of guides returned to camp with Jan and Adrian. Sadly, Adrian's injuries, and the jolting descent from the volcano, had proved too much for his 'indomitable spirit': he was found to be dead on arrival.

As the dramatic story unfolded, it was suggested that two lives might have been saved, and injuries possibly lessened, if the team had taken the precaution of wearing safety helmets and if information about Sangay's volcanic activity had been studied more closely. Later the matter was carefully considered by the expedition's writer, Professor Richard Snailham, who concluded that such precautions would not necessarily have been sufficient. Co-ordinating the rescue of the survivors, Lieutenant-Colonel John Blashford-Snell commented that 'the survival of four members of the expedition in such circumstances was a miracle.... It only emphasises the training of these men. They are very fit and tough explorers – some of the best in Britain.'[7]

The news of Adrian's death deeply affected those Society members who knew him and, while still feeling the full shock of the tragedy, we heard from Alan Cotterill that he was already trying to form 'Jock Trap 2' with members of the original team. He was probably correct in thinking that Adrian would have wanted it that way. Also the team members would soon be split up by new postings. However, things did not work out as hoped, personal circumstances preventing Alan's plans from being put into effect, and the caves were left without further investigation.

Shortly after Adrian's team returned to Bicester, Fast Castle was visited by members of the Royal Commission on Ancient Monuments. Their task, to produce a modern and definitive plan of the castle, was speedily but efficiently accomplished, and the results, although of little immediate significance to the current excavations, gave us for the first time an exact bird's eye view of the promontory. Drawn to a scale of 1:500, the Commission's survey appears to confirm the general accuracy of the medieval 1549 plan in relation to the size and layout of the castle buildings and two courtyards. The perimeter of the castle walls and the axis of the promontory, however, show a marked variation from the old plan which depicts the overall shape as being vaguely oblong, square onto the landmass. Except for the end point of the promontory, the shape is in fact almost triangular, and the rooms flanking the curtain wall are on a separate axis from the remainder of the buildings [Plate 23].[8]

As well as obtaining assistance from the Royal Commission, the Society was considerably indebted once more to Captain Powell for taking what were, as far as we know, the first close-up aerial photographs of the castle. This operation took place in mid-November 1976, and his report, entitled 'Flying Fast (or Building Castles in the Sky)', suggests that he found the trip exhilarating. Captain Powell's description of the flight begins with the somewhat unusual

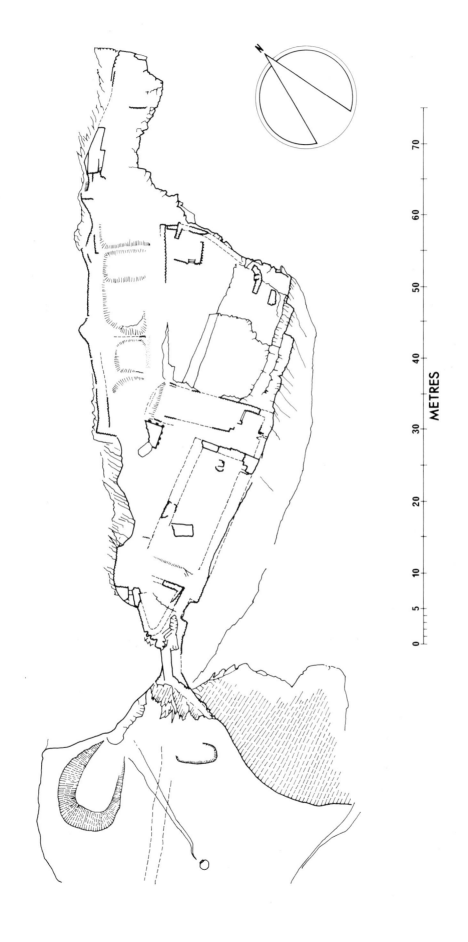

METRES

PLATE 23. Plan of Fast Castle, 1976.

question: 'Have you ever seen a large army officer struggling the fifty yards from an office to an aircraft with his parachute making him look like Dr. Scholl had transferred his allegiance to other areas of the anatomy?' Continuing, he replied that 'neither had Flight Lieutenant Mike Laundy, my driver, but it seemed to amuse him enough even without any rehearsal! Of such is RAF/Army co-operation made.' Having ensconced himself in the tandem-seated De Havilland Chipmunk, Captain Powell and his pilot then flew off to the wilds of Berwickshire for a cold photographic session high above the castle. His brief but amusing account relates that they

> had an interesting journey, flying first past my office (3rd from top row of windows at Edinburgh Castle) to which we seemed to look up, and then across country using the most advanced technique of aerial navigation known as 'follow the road'. Using a sextant and a few advanced calculations, we knew we had reached the right promontory by the shiny tin hut with flashing neon lights advertising 'La Société Caveau, Edinburgh'. Having got there, we felt that it would be foolish to go without taking pictures, thus back came the hood of the aircraft and in came a reminder as to why we wore three sweaters each. After a dummy run from WNW we made several passes over, around and seemingly under the castle, taking pictures from the most alarming angles. Mike then got bored so we climbed a few hundred feet, tipped over to the left and banked in a circle, 'snapping' as we went. My camera reflected the abject fear for as I recall, none of these came out.[9]

In fairness to Captain Powell's efforts, we should record that his colour photographs, although not produced to a professional standard, did in fact come out, and were more than adequate in portraying the rugged beauty of the sheer cliffs and crumbling ruins.

In June 1979 Professor Dennis Harding of Edinburgh University, following in the aerial footsteps of Captain Powell, took several photographs of the castle, in black-and-white as well as colour. Shot from a variety of angles, these superb pictures gave us an entirely new visual concept of Fast Castle, nestling at the bottom of Telegraph Hill [Plate 1].[10] The latest aerial survey was undertaken in 1980 by the Royal Commission on Ancient Monuments, and the resulting photographs, from very close range, illustrate the castle ruins with remarkable clarity [Plate 20].[11]

To continue our account of the excavations, work on the inner half of the lower courtyard began in 1971, and by 1974 most of the inclined trench beside the visitors' path was cleared out almost to bedrock. During our first season's work in this trench we uncovered a small stretch of downward-sloping bedrock, not far below the original surface, and situated near the central dividing line of the courtyard. The upper edge of the slope followed the direction of the bedrock fault lines towards the rock face which divides the castle into two levels. As digging continued it became evident that the edge, some 11 metres in length,[12] extended to join the rock face, but how far down did the slope reach? Judging by the depths of material removed from the outer courtyard, it was suggested that the rest of the inner courtyard probably had a maximum depth of about 1 metre. This seemed at the time a most satisfactory state of affairs, and it was assumed that excavations in this part of the castle would be completed by about 1976. How wrong we were, oh how wrong!

By 1974 our conjectures about the inner courtyard had been quite discredited, with the trench's depth exceeding the height of its excavators. Obviously work at the castle was going to be multiplied many times over, with no immediate end in sight. However, while our original estimates had proved over-optimistic, it still seemed possible that bedrock would soon be reached. Such is the foolishness of mere mortals! Little did we imagine the scale of the task which still lay ahead. If we had, Berwickshire would probably have seen the last of these amateur archaeologists. But the group was inspired to carry on by the site's excellent stratigraphy, the large number of interesting relics being found, the hope that perhaps we might after all discover the reputed connection between cave and castle, and a dogged determination to see the job through.

In 1974 the central portion of the inner courtyard was tackled for the first time and, as with the adjacent trench, excavation began to descend in an alarming manner. It is not possible within these pages to record the many problems which beset the excavators in their attempts to reach rock bottom. Suffice it to say that, year after year, we toiled our way through level after level of loam, clay, ash and rubble [Plate 22]. As we unwittingly neared the end of our quest, the depth reached became so great that it proved quite impossible to continue removing excavated material to the outer half of the courtyard. We literally ran out of energy and space, and it was necessary to create a spoil dump within a few inches of our work area. Finally, and with unbelievable relief, the last shovelful was excavated on Sunday 26 May 1985.[13] Our chairman Robin Murdoch made a few calculations to indicate the scale of the task completed during fifteen years of excavation within the inner courtyard: 'The dimensions of the area in question were approximately 15m by 10m by a maximum depth of 6.2m. Even allowing for the irregular nature of the bedrock floor, there was still in the region of 700 cubic metres of material removed. Given the proportions of soil and stone and their respective densities it is not unreasonable to allow one ton for each cubic metre. 700 tons by hand trowel is some scrape!'[14] Robin subsequently revised this estimate to 1,000 tons.

Several questions arise about the original function of this massive cavity and the circumstances under which the great quantities of midden material were dumped there, possibly over a long period. Although many problems of interpretation remain unresolved, one point seems clear from the datable finds recovered in the inner courtyard: quarrying operations must have formed part of at least one phase of construction work within the castle, not later than the early sixteenth century. This could be connected with a modernisation of the castle, possibly undertaken by Sir Patrick Home during the late fifteenth century, or the reputed rebuilding in 1521 by George, fourth Lord Home.

The masons and labourers working in this part of the quarry gained access to it by means of a narrow flight of steps, roughly cut out of the greywacke bedrock, which extended along the full length of the angular bedrock face. As each succeeding step was revealed by the excavation, like some descent into a newly-found Egyptian tomb, confidence began to grow amongst some of the diggers that we might well have stumbled across the long-lost entrance of the legendary stairway, carved through the castle rock down into the cave below. When the steps were found to terminate near the base of the rock face, there was naturally some degree of disappointment.

However, in 1979 hopes were raised once more when a large recess was discovered, hewn into the base of the rock face at its mid-point, directly below the upper level of the castle. Again we were disappointed, by finding that it extended only a few feet into the solid rock. Later reflection suggested that we might have discovered the basis of the stairway myth, without realising it at the time.

In considering its possible origins, we must examine the earliest known references to this delightful legend. As has already been mentioned, Alexander Carr was the source for all modern statements about the tradition, so the question arises: where did Carr get his information? One possible answer lies in a fictional account derived from the Gowrie Conspiracy of 1600, entitled *The Fatal Secret*. This apparently was written about 1835, its author unknown, and published in a series of short stories initiated by John Mackay Wilson, under the cumulative and celebrated title, *Wilson's Tales of the Borders*.[15]

The story revolves round Sir Robert Logan's notary or law agent, George Sprot and the succession of events leading to his execution in Edinburgh. The most interesting episode, so far as the legend is concerned, takes place when Logan and Sprot observe a large fishing boat approaching the castle with some of Logan's confederates on board. Their arrival is described thus: 'The sail of the boat was now lowered, and the vessel glided into the mouth of a huge cavern at the point of the castle rock. The knight hereupon conducted his visitor to the hall, where he left him, and descended to the cavern by a rude spiral stair-way, constructed in the heart of the cliff, to hear from his employees the result of their enterprise.'[16] Carr's description of the stair is almost identical to this passage and it seems likely that both versions were derived from the same source. Irrespective of who the original author was, it is necessary to ask whether the legend was a romantic creation or had indeed some basis in fact. Whatever the case, it is unlikely that the matter will ever be conclusively resolved, except by discovering the elusive passage. However, one theory which may shed some light on the problem deserves examination.

When the inner courtyard reverberated to the sounds of quarrying operations, it can be reasonably supposed that its existence was known to many of the local inhabitants. As the level was gradually raised with rubbish, perhaps over the space of two or three generations, a time would come when only the upper portion of the rock-cut steps were visible. Finally, the steps disappeared completely from view and, as memories began to fade, the original purpose of the quarry would be lost in the mists of time. Taking into account the dimensions of the inner courtyard, the nature of its initial use possibly formed a topic of neighbourhood conversation during the sixteenth century, with stories of its existence passing down from one generation to the next, particularly amongst the local farming population. The rock-cut steps of the inner courtyard might thus have come to be described as a rude spiral stairway by the embellishment of folk memory.

Half-way through the excavation the remains of a low, walled enclosure, contemporary with the earliest occupation level, were exposed to view in front of the large rock-hewn recess. Standing about 1 metre high on the uneven surface of a clay and rubble 'floor', and stretching approximately two-thirds of the way across the base of the inner courtyard, the wall was divided into two parts by a narrow entrance. The structure's function is not yet fully understood, but it appears to have been used for some time at least as a pen for small livestock, as suggested by the skulls of over twenty sheep found in the 'floor' level outside the enclosure. Further evidence in support of this interpretation came from a thick and evil-smelling deposit, covering a large area behind the wall. The smell of this 450 to 500 year-old manure, preserved by water-logging, defies description, and will long be remembered by those who had the 'privilege' of taking part in its excavation! However, this deposit proved an excellent source of finds, yielding large quantities of organic material, such as leather, textiles, and wood, that in normal conditions would not have survived.

The abundance and rich variety of interesting artefacts retrieved from such a small area was both fortunate and surprising. More than any other series of finds from the castle, they brought us into direct contact with the castle's medieval residents. Who used the leather belt or strap, with buckle holes and stitch marks as good as the day they were made? Why did somebody have to keep their shoes until the soles were almost completely worn through? The individual concerned must have had very sore feet indeed! The textiles found included fragments of homespun cloth, which still retains its khaki-coloured dye, and what appears to be the remnants of a child's glove, surely an item to strike an emotive chord. Perhaps the best example of the protection afforded to these objects by the layers which surrounded them is a silk lace with brass tag ends. Measuring 27 cms long, it is in almost perfect condition, and still capable of being used for its original purpose. From the wood recovered we have been able to identify several species of tree which presumably grew in the locality during the fifteenth and sixteenth centuries, including birch, juniper, oak and willow. Although a large proportion of this came in branch or twig form, many pieces, some of them quite large, still show the handiwork of the castle carpenters.

While animal bones form the bulk of the finds from the inner courtyard, the remainder are so diverse as to make even a brief summary impossible. To indicate the quantities involved, the 1976 finds register lists for that season's work a total of 3,082 finds, of which 2,511 are bone. Other items recovered over the years include bone awls, a candle, a door latch, a key, pins, a pair of scissors, two thimbles, and over twenty coins, mainly dating from the sixteenth century. On rare occasions an object of more than unusual interest or quality was unearthed. Such a discovery was normally followed by a jubilant exchange of congratulations and discussion of its archaeological and historical significance. Thus a plain but delicately carved bone chessman evoked thoughts of the countless hours spent by some of the castle occupants playing this age-old game. Two religious relics of undeniable aesthetic quality are a pilgrim's badge, dated to the last half of the fifteenth century, and a fifteenth-century Dutch pipeclay statuette of the Madonna and Child. Measuring just 7 cms in height, the features of this last item are so striking that they can only be fully appreciated when viewed under magnification [Plate 24]. Arguably the most beautiful and intricately designed object found in the inner courtyard, indeed throughout the whole period of our excavations at the castle, is an exquisitely-worked enamelled gold button of the late sixteenth or early seventeenth centuries [Plate 25]. The design consists of a central triangle and three pale green, enamelled leaves, surrounded by white, leafy scrolls, with a plain gold loop on the reverse side. The loss of this tiny item of jewellery, perhaps belonging to a member of the Home or Logan families, no doubt caused its original owner some annoyance, but its rediscovery proved that there was indeed 'Gold at Wolf's Crag'.

Two other parts of the castle received the attention of trowel and spade

72

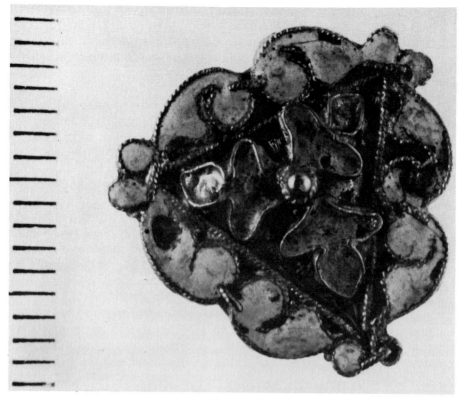

PLATE 24 (left). Madonna and Child, in pipeclay, Dutch, 15th century. Height: 7 cms.

PLATE 25 (above). Gold and enamel button, 16th–17th century. Diameter: 1.5 cms.

but, due to the considerable problems encountered in the inner courtyard, they had to be excavated in several stages. The first of these was a small room, some 4 by 6 metres, situated on the north-east corner of the upper level of the castle, adjacent to the keep and brewhouse, and designated by us as the kitchen. The foundation remains, as well as three distinct floor levels, suggest several phases of occupation, the earliest of which appears to have been contemporary with the deepest levels found in the lower courtyard. Apart from the perimeter wall foundations, a rude sandstone hearth was uncovered near the centre of the room, and a well-preserved sandstone drain was found venting through the east wall. On removing collapsed material from the south-west corner, including several large sandstone blocks, we were surprised to find the kitchen's main entrance, with its original threshold step and door-jamb base still in situ. The location of the entrance here corresponds almost exactly to the 1549 plan. In comparison with the lower courtyard, the kitchen produced only a few artefacts. These included a 'Bishop Kennedy penny', a decorated jet bead, and fragments of early clay pipes and window glass. Luckily, one piece of glass was found still inside its original lead surround, giving some indication of how the castle windows were glazed during the seventeenth century.

The last feature to be excavated was the well, located on the mainland not far from the entrance to the castle.[17] A trench measuring 6 by 9 metres was dug out around the well shaft, an exercise which established that there had been two successive occupation levels or walking surfaces in this area. Finds were even more sparse than in the kitchen. The most important include a James IV billon penny (1488-1513), and an iron key of generous proportions. Although now in a very fragile condition, the key is so large that it must have given its original keeper 'a definite list to starboard'. In 1986 a low curved stone wall was uncovered about half way between the well head and the base of the adjacent hill. An occupation level at the base of this wall yielded several pieces of very coarse Iron Age pottery. The wall may therefore be part of an Iron Age round house, reused later, when the castle's well was constructed, as a revetment against the hill slope.

As part of the same excavation, a concerted effort was also put into clearing the well shaft itself, which seemed unlikely to be more than 3 or 4 metres deep. Pumping water out by normal means was quite impracticable, so we resorted instead to siphoning. Our first experiments with garden hose pipes failed, but eventually the method proved effective, when we had bought several reels of heavy-duty industrial hose, made of a red plastic which became the favourite diet for the local rodent population. Less than a month after our project's completion much of the tubing, left in the storage hut, had been almost completely eaten through. Thus the shaft could be excavated, initially to a depth of 6 feet or 1.83 metres. In this first phase, the well was found to be packed with rubble, suggesting that it had been deliberately backfilled. There were also layers of silt and muck, containing many pieces of wood, often still with its bark. Before continuing further, it was necessary to shore the shaft with sheets of corrugated iron and stout wooden beams, both as a safety precaution and to gain access to the well's nether regions. The reinforcing materials, along with other heavy equipment, were manhandled from the car park by means of 'slave labour' and a modified golf caddy, to prepare for a weekend's intensive effort in late August 1986, when the rest of the well was cleared out.

I had long wanted to camp for the night at Fast Castle, so, taking advantage of this golden opportunity, on the Saturday afternoon I followed a fellow excavator's example by pitching my tent at the base of the hill, a few yards from the well. This operation was not as easy as it sounds, the sloping surface of the tufted grass and undulating bedrock making the task ten times harder than usual. The situation was made even worse by my lack of experience in this form of 'entertainment', and the final result of my efforts, although quite functional, brought forth hilarious comments from my family who visited the site the next day. After a few hours' work Saturday night fell and, as twinkling lights appeared along the Firth of Forth, the remains of the old castle faded into darkness. Unable to resist the temptation to inspect the ruins in their eerie yet peaceful darkened solitude, I ventured warily amongst the time-worn stones. During this tour of inspection, the scene was made even more dramatic by the flashing beams of the St. Abbs lighthouse, which pierced the gloom and bounced off the keep wall with pulsating regularity.

The next day dawned for me at 6.30 a.m., thanks to my camping partner who had already been up for an hour. By mid-morning, when the rest of the crew arrived, a further 3 feet or nearly 1 metre had been excavated, and it was suspected that bedrock would soon be reached. This was indeed the case and, by the end of the day, the well's base had been uncovered, drawn and photographed. With some satisfaction we measured the depth of the well shaft at 3.78 metres (12 feet 5 inches), matching almost exactly our original estimate. To ensure that nothing of interest escaped our attention, every bucket of silt and muck was carefully riddled, a nauseous and almost completely unrewarding process. The only artefacts found in this 'gunge' were several pieces of shaped timber, and a lead disc, a very disappointing haul. It had been confidently expected that pottery and at least one or two coins would turn up from somewhere in the shaft. Either the castle occupants were extremely careful and thrifty in their use of the well, or, more probably, it was cleaned out shortly before ceasing to function as a water supply. The task of backfilling the well shaft with rubble occupied the next day, and shortly thereafter the trench was landscaped.

A few weeks later, on Sunday 12 October 1986, the last shovelful of bedrock rubble was excavated from the kitchen, an historic event for the Society after sixteen years' work at the castle. The significance of the moment was not lost on those present, and two stalwarts were duly photographed for posterity, along with the loaded 'ceremonial' shovel. When congratulations and handshakes had been exchanged, all those who had taken part in the excavations over the years were toasted with our national drink. Thus ended what perhaps may prove to be Scotland's longest-running amateur archaeological dig.

Now that this part of our mammoth undertaking is at last concluded, we have had to consider the possibility of future excavations at the castle. However, any renewed activity there will depend on settling a number of organisational problems. It will also be necessary to obtain permission from the site's owner and from the Scottish Development Department (Historic Buildings and Monuments Directorate), which listed the castle as a Scheduled Monument in 1981. The outlook is therefore very uncertain. In the meantime we have enough backroom work on hand to keep the Society occupied for several years. During 1986 our historical research team began the complicated task of sifting through a mass of information on the castle's early history. The period under review runs from the twelfth to the mid-sixteenth century and, if all goes according to plan, the results should appear within the next two or three years. Two excavation reports have already been published on the castle well, and very soon a publication on the kitchen should be forthcoming. However, no definite completion date can be set for the report on the lower courtyard, because so much evidence still requires analysis.

Every year throughout the excavation, it was our policy to deposit all notable finds into the care of the former National Museum of Antiquities of Scotland (now Royal Museum of Scotland). With the co-operation of Dr. David Caldwell, and the expertise of the laboratory staff, objects such as wood, leather, and certain categories of metal, received suitable conservation treatment. In January 1985 most of the other finds were brought into the Museum, and the time-consuming task of classification and analysis began in earnest. To judge from the reactions of those taking part in this project, its most popular, indeed therapeutic, aspect has been the sorting out and assembling of pottery 'jigsaws'. The results, although not spectacular, have included the partial reconstruction of seventeen vessels, ranging in size from a 38 cms high earthenware container to a small drinking cup. With many finds specialist analysis is naturally of prime importance for increasing our knowledge of late-medieval life at Fast Castle. A study of the coins has been undertaken by David Caldwell and Nicholas Holmes, Edinburgh City Archaeologist. Dennis Gallagher has produced a report on the clay pipe fragments, and the bones are currently being analysed by Lin Barnetson at Oxford. Clearly, however, it will be many years before all the finds have yielded their secrets and our labours are concluded.

Overleaf: PLATE 26. Conjectural reconstruction of Fast Castle as it might have appeared in the 16th century, by David Simon.

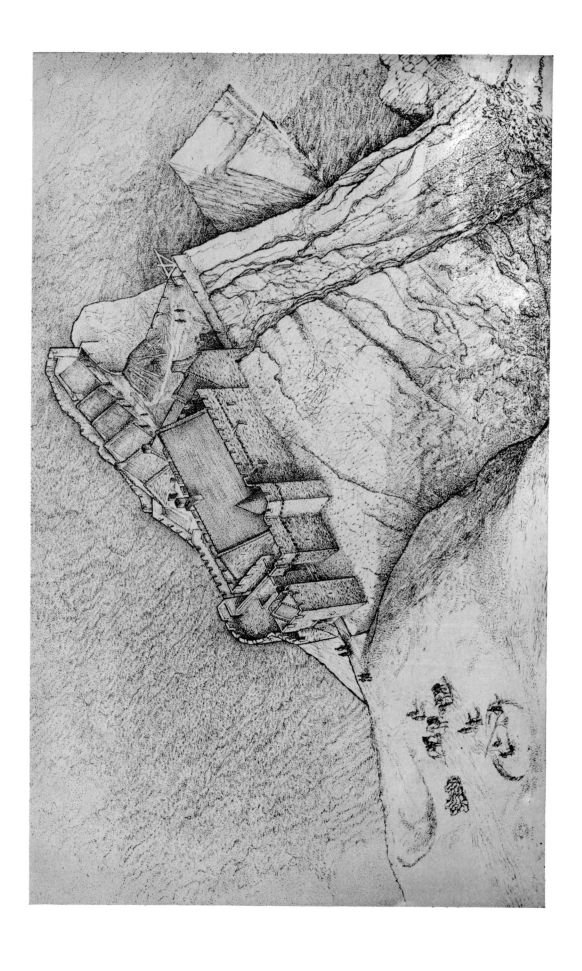

Appendix 1

A Conjectural Illustration of Fast Castle

By David Simon

Fast Castle today is little more than a scatter of enigmatic grass-grown lumps in the ground and a few stumps of masonry, occupying a bleak promontory jutting into the North Sea [Plate 18]. The headland is just one of a number of ancient cliff castle and promontory fort sites along this stretch of the Berwickshire coast. Its longevity and high degree of development as a fortified place is due to the strength of its position, surrounded as it is on the seaward side by cliffs up to 150 feet high and connected to the mainland by a narrow neck.

One of the first things the visitor sees on approaching the causeway to the promontory is a curved masonry wall overlooking a ditch and containing the remains of a splayed gun loop. Further on, past a massive upturned conglomerate of stone and mortar, one of the two remaining pieces of wall still standing to almost full height can be seen at the edge of the crag. Beyond this, with a range of grass-grown terrace-like foundations to one side and a quarry-like hole to the other, the path leads to the end of the promontory where, next to a massive surviving piece of curtain wall, further progress is arrested by a breathtaking 100 foot drop to the mouth of a large sea cave.

Here at the cliff edge, surrounded by the echoing cries of fulmars high above a rough sea, the sense of the place's remoteness and wildness is strongest. It now seems a strange site for human habitation. After the climb down from Dowlaw, and certainly after the climb back up again, it appears utterly inaccessible. Who lived here? Who built the castle and when? Above all, what did it look like?

At first the task of interpreting the fragmentary remains and establishing a coherent mental picture of Fast Castle before its destruction seems impossible. Fortunately, what is left of the fabric can yield important clues to the structure's original appearance, and even more fortunately a sixteenth-century plan of the castle survives, one of the earliest known for any Scottish fortification. This survey, when examined alongside a modern plan of the existing remains, gives a much clearer idea of the building's layout. The knob of masonry containing the gun loop at the landward end of the promontory is shown at one corner of what was a triangular structure, now almost completely lost on the ground. Flanking this on its south-east side was an outer gatehouse, the foundations of which can still be seen along the side of the crag. A second inner gatehouse shows up one of a number of anomalies in the sixteenth-century plan. It is depicted as a much wider structure than the outer gate, but its foundations on site follow the same line. Further anomalies in the work of the 1549 draughtsmen show with the square shape they have made of the castle complex; in reality the site is triangular. Apart from these differences, the ancient plan shows details for which no traces now remain.

Care has been taken to represent the walkway across the ditch and between the two gatehouses as consisting of transverse planks, but the portion immediately in front of the outer gate is drawn in such a way as to suggest a drawbridge. Details such as the flight of steps within the triangular work giving access to an upper level and the internal arrangements of the hall and chamber are now gone forever.

Taken together with the results of excavation, the ancient and modern plans supply ample evidence for the ground plan of Fast Castle. Projecting this plan into elevations presents greater difficulty. The one piece of evidence for the height of the hall and chamber is the piece of masonry still standing to the corbel table, a height of 17 feet, at the eastern corner. This structure's internal face reveals the beginning of a sandstone vault, the ceiling of the hall and chamber. The corbels at the wall head would have carried the crenellated parapet surrounding an attic storey under the high pitched roof. Future excavations may well reveal a basement level within this building, an abbreviated tower house.

An interesting feature on the 1549 plan is the presence of two stairways in the south-east wall of the hall and chamber, one a straight flight possibly descending to the basement and the other a circular stair accommodated within a buttressed wall section. I have assumed that the circular stairway gave access to the attic and wall-walk. On site the turf covering has been disturbed at the point where this stair seems to have been, and amongst the rubble a wedge-shaped piece of sandstone can be seen, possibly one of the steps.

The levels for the main entrance to the castle have proved the most problematic to reconstruct, but luckily some evidence survives. The upper surface of the rubble infill above the inner gatehouse foundations forms a flat surface which seems to represent the floor of the entrance passage some eight or nine feet below the level of the corbel table. I consider that both inner and outer gateways were probably quite small, and that the lintel of the inner gate was roughly at the same level as the corbel table. Under normal circumstances this arrangement would seem dangerously low in a fortification. However, the precipitous approach (the timber gangway between the outer and inner gatehouses juts over a 150 foot drop), the fact that it was an *inner* gatehouse, and the known sixteenth-century tendency to build low, dissuade me from arbitrarily increasing the height of the parapet [Plate 26].

The level of the approach to the outer gate would originally have been much higher than that commanded at present by the gun loop in the curved wall. Evidently a timber or stone structure would have bridged the ditch and probably, on the evidence of the sixteenth-century plan, stopped short of the outer gate to allow for the drawbridge. Drawbridges had a long vogue and it is reasonable to assume that there was one at Fast in the sixteenth century. The means of raising a drawbridge has a bearing on an interpretation of the superstructure of the outer gatehouse. The entrance doorway being quite small, a correspondingly small drawbridge could have been raised by windlass alone without the aid of gaffes and counterweights. I have reconstructed the outer gate tower as being of sufficient height to accommodate a room over the passage to house the windlass, with a crenellated parapet and cap house above this.

In the absence of evidence to the contrary, it seems likely that the height of the triangular work and the curved structure adjoining it would have matched that of the hall and chamber block with the stair, noted earlier on the 1549 plan, probably giving access to a flat platform, perhaps timber-built, at parapet level.

The western flank of the promontory was bounded along its full length by a curtain wall [Plate 19] which, if the surviving piece can be regarded as typical, was possibly 15 or 20 feet high to the wall-walk and about 4-5 feet wide. In the sixteenth-century plan it is shown as following a straight line, but must in fact have been quite irregular, rising up the sloping promontory in a series of steps. About half way along the wall a rectangular bastion is shown, the remains of which can be traced on the ground, together with the footings of a small square building, tucked inside its northern end. This building, no more than a single room, is shown on the old plan as entered from the bastion down a short flight of steps. Beyond it more rooms were built against the inside of the curtain wall forming a series like a terraced street. The one at the end of the promontory must have been exceedingly narrow, probably having a lean-to roof, while it is likely that on the upper four the roofs were pitched. A passageway between rooms four and five, the lowest in the series, led to a postern gate that gave access to the flank of the promontory. At the very end of the site, next to the lowest room, a garderobe is shown on the 1549 plan.

From the end of the promontory a lesser wall followed the north-east edge of the lower courtyard to the crane. In mild weather a boat can easily put in to the mouth of the sea cave 100 feet below and the crane would have been an efficient way of bringing supplies and materials into the heart of the castle. However, in choppy conditions this operation would be dangerous, for the cave mouth then becomes a cauldron of white water. Remains possibly associated with the crane have been uncovered at the eastern corner of the lower courtyard, in particular an area of pavement which could be part of the stance from which it was worked. At its southern end the lower courtyard contains a large pit, no doubt representing a quarry from which part of the castle fabric was obtained [Plate 22].

Above this, adjoining the north-east gable of the hall, stood the kitchen and brewhouse. Their internal layout is drawn on the sixteenth-century plan, and probably they were gable-roofed with slates. The south-east flank of the lower courtyard shows no evidence on the ground of ever having been walled, but the sixteenth-century plan shows a continuation of the perimeter wall along the edge of the cliff, at this point almost completely sheer.

The site of Fast Castle has an elusive quality. Even from the top of nearby Telegraph Hill [Plate 17] it is difficult to judge clearly the lie of the land, because the promontory surface shelves away so steeply. Only by looking at aerial photographs in conjunction with the plans can the site be really appreciated. Although it appears to be heavily overlooked from neighbouring high land, much of the interior is hidden and would originally have been screened completely by the southern facade of the castle enclosing the highest point of the promontory.

At some time a ditch and bank were dug enclosing a sector of the mainland nearest the promontory. They form a curve running from cliff to cliff and crossing the crown of Hawksheugh. The southern end stops short of the cliff edge where the pathway to the castle passes between a ravine and a rock face. Nothing is known about this ditch and bank and no excavation work has been done on them, but probably they constituted a defensive palisade enclosing an outer ward. Within this ward lies the only source of fresh water that we have been able to locate. Presumably the area also accommodated various outbuildings – workshops, stables, and storehouses – for which there would not have been room on the cramped promontory itself. It is not possible to say with certainty over what period this outer defence work existed, but I feel that it was an integral part of the fortress, both to control the high ground and the castle approach.

My illustrations are conjectural reconstructions of Fast Castle as it might have looked during the sixteenth century. They reflect the opinions of the many people with whom I have spoken during the research work. The conclusions reached cannot be definitive, for we will never know how the place really looked, but they are as true to the available evidence as I could make them. Their preparation has involved a study of the site, assisted by the archaeologists who have partially excavated it, and by their accumulation of photographs, plans, notes and sketches, together with details drawn from other Scottish sites. In the tentative preliminary drawings the range of forms that the superstructure could have taken were explored and developed, pared down or eliminated as seemed appropriate. Eventually a number of drawings containing the kernel of a reconstruction emerged, forming the basis of the final pieces. An important consideration, however, has been to avoid too clinical a result, for Fast Castle has a peculiar fascination and a powerful atmosphere. I have tried to incorporate something of these qualities into the drawings.

Appendix 2

Documents Illustrating Local Life in the Eighteenth and Nineteenth Centuries

[From the Hall of Dunglass Estate Ledgers (Scottish Record Office, GD 206)]

(a) **Thatching at Dowlaw, 1750**

GD 206 5/37

Receipt Anderson to Sir John Hall for Thatching at Dowlaw

Dunglass 13th Novr 1750 Recd from Sir John Hall of Dunglas Bart., Twelve pound, ten shillings Scots money for twenty five Days thatching at Dowlaw by my father George Anderson deceased, at ten pence pr Day, by mr. William anderson his Son Indweller in Auldhamstocks: To witness whereof I have subscribed these presents written by Robert Hogg Schoolmaster in Cockburnspath place, Day, Moneth, & Year of God, above set down Before these witnesses said Robert Hogg, and Stephen Redpath Tenant in Saltpanhall

Robt. Hogg witness
Stephen Readpath witness

(b) **Farming at Redheugh: John Wauchope to Sir John Hall, 1764**

GD 206 2/278

Redheugh 1st Aprile 1764

Sir

I saw Mr. Watson this day who told me you desire me to make a Reasonable demand, and if you thought it To you would aggrie to it. I really cannot Depend To much upon my own Judgement as to make any Demand, I would much rather refer it to yourself, but if you want that I shoud make any demand I hope youll give me a little time to consult some persons of better skill than myself. You was pleased to say in your last you thought I had been managing the farm as all Tenants that are to Remove do. I am Confident were you to look at the grounds you would change your opinion. I never doubted but you knew the prestations in my Tack as well as I did myself, nor did I ever value myself on Inclosing any part of the land though I believe the Inclosures at Redheugh contain near double the Quantity of land I am Obliged to Inclose. All the Neighbours here know very well in what situation I got both farms and the Inclosing is the least part of the expence in putting them in the order they are in at present. I never had any corn in Windilaws hill within these three years except what the Sheep folded, and when I got it there was not a bit of the outfield had lain above three years and every bit of the Infield in Corn and in bad order not to mention a single Rigg in faugh nor a Shovel full of Dung.

Allow me to observe that no Tenat lays out Infield eight or nine years in Grass without Taking the Benefit of 3 or 4 Crops after it has lain To long unless there be an express Clause in his Tack to the Contrary. My wife Begs her Compliments to Miss Hall and you and I am Respectfull

        Sir
          your most obed: Lord

          John Wauchope

(c) Survey of Dowlaw, 1771   GD 206 5/232

The following is the Barony of Dowlaw
Measured in Spring 1771 ....
Laid down by a Scale of four English Chains in the Inch
The Houses, yeards, and Roads, of the following Farms
are Included & are all surface measure ....
      (signed) Jas Watson

Barrony of Dowlaw ....

	Farm of Cauldside............................			Acr Parts
A	Arrable			90,855
B	Muir			29,732
	Sea Braes Including Lancies Bank			17,570
	....			138,157

	Farm of Kingshill			Acr Parts
A	Muir and some Arrable			60,874
B	Arrable Including some pieces of Muir			117,949
	The whole Sea Braes of Ditto Farm			19,020
	....			197,843

	Farm of Cairn-shot & Eastfield...............			Acr Parts
A	....			90,429
	Sea Braes of Ditto			11,218
B	The Park Including Sea Braes and Braes upon Lumsdon Burn			51,151
	....			152,798

	Farms of Abate law &c			Acr Parts
A	Abate-law			33,521
B	Miln-land		29,170	
	Braes of Ditto		3,753	32,923
C	Part of Dowlaw Infield P:A:A:			32,154
D	Kirk Bank		37,316	
	Braes of Ditto		3,463	40,779
E	Smiths Park & Void ground			4,000

F Farehill Including some Muir		49,637	
G Black side		29,018	
Braes of Ditto		1,027	30,045
....			223,059

Part of Dowlaw Outfield	Acr Parts
A Dowlaw Outfield P:A:A:	73,833
B Muir East of Old Stone Dyke......................	30,000
C Muir West & South of Old Stone Dyke	70,832
....	174,665
D Disputed	2,200

(d) Horses on the Farms of Old Cambus, 1792

GD 206 5/64

Jannuary 1st 1792. An Account of the whole number of Horses on the farms of Auld Cambus Being the property of Sir James Hall Bart of Dunglas and their valuations

	Horses	Mares	£	s	
Black Whitefoot	1	–	19	–	
Bay Rob	1	–	13	–	
Gray Blue	1	–	7	10	Sold at Dou
Gray Mason	1	–	18	–	law Sale 1792
Black Ball	1	–	17	–	
Bay Rose	–	1	17	–	
Black Jane	–	1	20	–	
Chestnut Nell	–	1	13	–	
Black Sharper	1	–	20	–	
Yellow Hempy	1	–	18	–	
White Farmer	1	–	11	–	
Long Tailed Bay	1	–	16	–	
Old Black	1	–	13	–	
Bay Smiler	1	–	15	–	
Bay Snippy	1	–	17	–	
Black Dick	1	–	5	–	Sold at Doulaw sale
The old Dunglass Horse punch	1	–	3	–	Shot by the order of Sir James
Black Plowman	1	–	15	–	
old Riptured White Captain	1	–	5	–	Died March 1793 sold Skin

(e) Extracts from the Farm Accounts of Dowlaw, 1792-4   GD 206 5/26,67

1792		£	s	d
May 28	to Custom for 2 Horses at Dowlaw Roup Selling	0	6	1
Jun 11	Bed Cloaths for Dowlaw Husbandmen	1	5	8
Aug 8	Sandy maclain & c. for moving 17 1/2 acres at Dowlaw at 2 pr	1	15	
Oct 27	To James Hailstanes Dowlaw one Cow for winter Milck	6	10	

1793				
Jan 10	To Thos Christie Dunbar for 20 Bags for Dowlaw	2	3	4
Feb 12	paid for Coals to the Servants of auld Cambus & Dowlaw	1	17	7
12	6 Cart Loads of Coals from Berwick to Boil corn at Dowlaw & auld Cambus		17	4
Apr 24	Meal to the Servants at Dowlaw & West Mains	6		
Jun 23	To Thos Guiler for thathing 2 Houses at Dowlaw	4	4	3
Jul 16	To the Backer of Coldingham for bread to the plowmen when at Dowlaw macking Bear & Turnop Seed	6	19	4
16	To the Brewer of Coldingham for ale for the above work	6	14	8
Sep 2	Joiner Work done by the piece at Dowlaw	1	17	2
Oct 6	To James Hardy wodend for Beer to mowers & Doulaw howers		7	4
16	To poor rates paid Doulaw for one year Ending May 31=94	4	4	10
31	Auld Cambus & Dowlaw Day Labour	34	19	6
Nov 4	To John Kinghorn for a Grindstone for Doulaw		7	3
29	To Wm Stannes and partners for Draining at Doulaw	21	9	8
29	To wages & Board Wages for the Servants at Auldcambus & Dowlaw for Half a Year	35	16	
30	From Auld Cambus & Dowlaw Day Labour Book	22	6	4
Dec 4	To Mr. Paxton Berwick for Candels for attending the Cattle at West Mains & Doulaw	1	4	2
27	To John Sleigh for Straw to thath at Dowlaw straw			

1794				
Jan 20	By Tho Guiler for thathing New work at Dunglass & repairing at Doulaw	4	8	9
31	By Auldcambus & Doulaw Daylabour Book	14	8	10
Apr 23	By Mr. Renton Eyemouth for Window Tax for Dowlaw & West mains	2	17	7
May 26	By George Hog Wright at Doulaw for repairing utensels when working there		13	8
31	Auld Cambus & Doulaw Daylabour Book	1	13	4
Jul 30	By Alex France Coldingham for Bread to plowmen Sundry Times working at Doulaw		5	
	By Peter Fair Coldingham for ale to plowmen Sundry Times working at Dowlaw		5	

Sep	17	By Meal at Auldcambus & Dowlaw for Hay leading Building & Harvest	3 16
	17	By pairing Land at Doulaw and the allotment of Common	12 15 6
	27	By Charles McKinzie Dunbar for Tiles to Repair the Roofs at Doulaw & workmanship	2 4 6
Oct	22	By Ale for work people at Dowlaw & Harvest at westmains & Doulaw	7 15 11
		By Bread for work people Doulaw & Harvest west mains & Doulaw	8 13 11
Nov	3	By Coals to the Hinds & Hirds at Dowlaw & west maines & Gates lowand & Custom	4 8 2
Dec	12	By pantyles 720 at 6 Shilling per Hundred for Dowlaw	2 3 2

(f) A Funeral at Cockburnspath Church, 1795

GD 206 5/103

November 20   To expenses from the funeral of a Woman cast
in by the sea and buried in Cockburnspath
Church Yard 11/1 viz – Wrights making the
Coffin 2/4 – men at funeral 3/6 –
Day Book To Black. 6d – cords 3d – Whisky 2/- –
Grave-digger 2/6

N.B. Wood for the coffin & a winding sheet
was got from Dunglass

(g) Shipwrecks, 1835

GD 206 5/236

Shipwrecks
: On Monday the 19th day of January of this year three Vessels were wrecked on the Shores of the Dunglass Estate belonging to Sir John Hall, Bart.

Sloop
: One betwixt Redheugh & Dowlaw. Coal Laden & all Hands perished the only thing found by which her name could be known was a piece of the Stern with 'The Brothers' of Banff painted on it.

Schooner
: Named 'Niele' of Montrose. Captain & two of the Crew drown'd. Came on Shore immediately below the Preventive Station at Redheugh, Coal Laden.

Schooner
: 'William Davidson' of Thurso Captain James Ritchie Master. A description of the circumstances that took place during the storm & till the Crew got on Shore follows in the Captains own words of writing:-

About two o'clock on monday afternoon, when by our reckoning we were about ten miles N.E. by N. of St. Abbs Head, we were overtaken by a gale of wind from N.E., so heavy that before we could get our sails furled, some of them were blown to pieces, spars broken, bulwarks completely washed away, the vessel labouring in the trough of the sea, and almost covered with water, so that she became quite unmanageable, and all endeavours of the crew to make the vessel lye easy in the sea were fruitless.

Knowing that we were driving very fast down on a lea shore, although we could see no land, owing to the darkness of the night, & continual showers of snow, and considering that the only chance of saving our lives would be to run the vessel on shore while it was high water, we hoisted a small sail called the forestay sail, by means of which the vessel steered before the wind.

We then saw dimly through the snow & spray the High cliffs of Billsdean, and the waves breaking tremendous to a considerable distance from the shore; the vessel enters the breakers & strikes, a dreadful crash, comes broadside on to the rocks, every ray of hope is excluded. The crew cling to the rigging, while the vessel drives nearer & nearer to the cliffs. At length after being dashed about for some time, & successively swept over by the waves the vessel lies still, & the tide receding, the crew got landed by means of swinging themselves with a backstay from the main topmast head

to the cliff when they were fortunately landed on the
extremity of a gravell walk leading towards Billesdean
& made by order of Sir John Hall, Bart. Had it not
been for which they must have perished with cold after
they had landed.

J.W. Ritchie

(h) **Extracts from the Farm Accounts of Dowlaw, 1853–60**

GD 206 5/29,30

			£	s	d
1853					
Sep	23	By A W Purvis Dunse for County Rates for the Lands of Dowlaw including contribution to the H. & A. Society of Scotland	9	4	6
1854					
Sep	28	To Mr Cowe Dowlaw	10		
1855					
Jan	22	By Daniel Hossick Wright C'Path for Repairing Cottages Dowlaw	3	13	
1857					
Jun	21	By Mr Crawford Dunse County Rates for Dowlaw	5	5	
Sep	22	To Mr Cowe Dowlaw for Net Stobs	8	4	
1858					
Aug	26	By Ordnance Survey Sheets of Dowlaw Farm	12		
Sep	9	By Danl Hossick, CoPath Acct of Estimate for Wright Work of Cottages at Dowlaw Farm	117		
		Danl Hossick Wright Co'Path for setting up new Trowse Manger &c in Stable at Dowlaw	15	10	
Oct	9	Danl Hossick Co Path to Acct of Estimate of Wright Work of Cottages at Dowlaw	20		
Dec	1	Daniel Hossick Co'Path to acct of Estimate of Wright Work for Hinds Houses Dowlaw	20		
1859					
Feb	5	To Messers Tods Maray & Jamieson [Hall's solicitors] Contra payments	680		
Jan	6	A Crawford Dunse County Rates for the Barony of Co'path	81	5	3
		Do Do for Dowlaw	7	17	6
Feb	12	Wright Work of Cottages at Dowlaw	77		
		To Danl Hossick Wright Co'path for repairs on Dowlaw Farm House	30	11	3

	Do Do for repairs on Dowlaw Granary & for new Hog Houses	2	16	6
Mar 11	Jas Paterson Slater Co Path Balance of Estimate of Slater & Plaster Work of Cottages at Dowlaw	15	10	
	Do Do for repairs on Dowlaw Farm House & Roofing two Pig Houses	4	2	6
	By Jas Smith Mason, Birnieknowes Balance of Estimate for Building Cottages at Dowlaw	61		
	Jas Smith Birnieknowes for repairs on Dowlaw Farm House	5		
	Do Do for Building Pig Houses at Dowlaw	11	9	
Aug 25	By Ths Dickson to acct of Building Stone Dykes on Dowlaw Farm	7		
Sep 28	Mr. Cowe Dowlaw for oats	18		
Oct 11	By Ths Dickson to acct of Building Dykes Dowlaw Farm	12		
Dec 21	By Ths Dickson to Acct of Building Dykes on the Farm of Dowlaw	10		

1860

Jan 24	By Wm Brodie Seafield for Tiles & Bricks	19	13	2
	Do Do Tiles & Bricks for cottages for Dowlaw	14		
Mar 9	By James Paterson, to Acct of Slater Work Dowlaw Farm Offices	12	10	
Mar 26	By Jas Smith Mason, Birnieknowes to Acct of Building Sheds at Dowlaw	30		
Apr 20	Jas Paterson, Co Path, Balance of Acct of Slater Work on Dowlaw Farm Offices	7	2	
21	By Jas Smith, Mason, Balance of acct for Building and repairing Farm offices Dowlaw	40	10	
	Do Do Estimate for Building dykes, Pig Houses, and Coal House, at Dowlaw	34	8	10
May 9	By Ths Dickson, Chirnside, Balance of Estimate for Building Dykes on Dowlaw Farm	27	2	
Jul 6	By John McNaught, to Acct of Building Dykes at Dowlaw Farm	5		
Jul 21	By John McNaught to Acct of Building Dykes on the Farm of Dowlaw	7		
Aug 29	By John McNaught, to Acct of Building Dykes on Dowlaw Farm, Paid on 9th	2	10	
Oct 19	By Cash paid by Mr Cowe, to R Nicolson & Son, Plumbers for Spouts for Dowlaw per Acct	5	4	8
23	By John McNaught for Building Dykes on Dowlaw Farm	1	7	6
Nov 7	By Jas Smith, Mason, CoPath Etc...			
	Do Do for repairing Stock Yard Dyke Dowlaw	3	11	10

Appendix 3

The Ornithology of the Berwickshire Coastline, from St. Abbs to Siccar Point, in the Nineteenth Century

[From George Muirhead, *The Birds of Berwickshire* (2 vols., Edinburgh, 1895)]

Black Tailed Godwit

It is very rarely seen in Berwickshire, the only instance of its occurrence in the county known to me being that of a specimen which was shot at Dowlaw, near Fast Castle, by Mr. William Cowe about 1864, and which is preserved in the collection of Mr. Peter Cowe, Lochton.

Chough

The late Dr. George Johnston, of Berwick-on-Tweed, in his address to the Berwickshire Naturalists' Club, at its first Anniversary Meeting, on the 19th of September 1832, says '....I must not leave this majestic coast without mention of another of its feathered tenants, the Cornish Chough, which indeed was not seen by us on this occasion, but is certainly ascertained to breed in the rocks between St. Abb's and Fast Castle. This fact, distinctly mentioned by Bishop Lesly in his history *De Origine Scotorum*, published about 300 years ago, has been overlooked or disregarded by naturalists, who have considered the bird peculiar to the western shores of Britain.' ....In 1846, Mr. Hardy noted that a pair were then at Fast Castle, and that the young used formerly to be climbed for, and taken out of the nests to be tamed.

Mr. Archibald Hepburn, in a paper 'On some of the Mammalia and Birds found at St. Abb's Head' in 1851, says that 'the Chough or Red-legged Crow is now extinct, except a solitary pair' which, according to his information, 'seldom strayed far from Fast Castle, a few miles to the eastward of the Head.' ....The Chough appears to have become extinct about St. Abb's Head and Fast Castle between 1846 and 1855, and to have remained so; for had this not been the case, the bird would surely have been seen after the last-mentioned date by fishermen and others.

Eider Duck

Mr. Hardy, Oldcambus, who, in his papers on the local migration of birds in the History of the Berwickshire Naturalists' Club, frequently notices the occurrence of this duck off the coast about Siccar Point from November to May, says: 'They utter a noise like the cooing of a Pigeon, and the fishermen call them Cud-doos. They stay all the winter, but are seldom seen off here, and are said to breed in some of the rocks near Fast Castle.'

Herring Gull

This Gull is more plentiful on the sea-coast of Berwickshire than any other kind, and is found there at all seasons of the year. It is, however, to be seen in the greatest numbers about St. Abb's Head, where its harsh, cackling cries fill the air during the breeding season.

Rounding the point at Fast Castle we see the Black Mask Rock with a number of Herring Gulls' nests upon it, and still keeping westwards we pass Geddes' Haven and the Little Rooks, and then we reach the Gull Rock and Maw Craig, near the mouth of the Wolden Lee Burn, the most westerly breeding places of the Herring Gull on the Berwickshire coast. This point is about three-quarters of a mile to the west of Fast Castle.

This Gull is, however, occasionally found breeding further westwards. Mr. Hardy notes, under date 30th June 1886: 'A Herring Gull's nest was found yesterday by Professor Lebour's pupils on the rocks near Siccar – between it and Redheugh.'

Kestrel

It frequents the precipitous rocks on the sea-coast of Berwickshire, where it breeds, some of its favourite nesting places being near Siccar Point, Fast Castle, Blakey, and the Coal Point at Lamberton.

Martin

While the Chimney Swallow confines itself wholly to our buildings for the site of its nest, great numbers of our Martins continue to build in the situations which they would occupy long before there were any houses in Berwickshire, such as against the sides of the rocky caverns and precipitous cliffs of the sea-coast, from Swallow Craig, near Oldcambus, round by Fast Castle and St. Abb's Head, to the neighbourhood of Burnmouth.

Peregrine Falcon

Mr. Robert Cowe, Oldcastles, who lived at Dowlaw for many years, has informed me that, from 1839 to 1850, it nested regularly every season near Fast Castle; and Mr. Archibald Hepburn, who contributed many interesting notes to Macgillivray's *History of British Birds*, records in 1850 that 'four pairs of the Peregrine Falcon breed on the coast of Berwickshire; one at Burnmouth, one at Petticowick Cove to the west of St. Abb's, one at Ernesheugh, and a fourth at Fast Castle.'

My friend Mr. Hardy, Oldcambus, writes that the Peregrine nested at Halternsloup near Coldingham Shore in 1836 and 1853, and has occasionally bred in a steep, massive rock, a short distance to the east of Rammel Cove, since 1856. He adds that it had its eyrie at Fast Castle, Whiteheugh, and near Burnmouth, in 1857, and that it was from the last-mentioned locality that Mr. Baird of Newbyth sometimes got his Falcons.

Two pairs of Falcons appear to have bred in the vicinity of St. Abb's Head in 1859, and in 1860 there was a nest in the precipice at Hawksheugh immediately to the east of Fast Castle, which seems to have been occupied on the 3rd of May 1865, when I visited that part of the coast with Mr. William Cowe, Dowlaw, who showed me the cliff at Hawksheugh up which his brother, Mr. Peter Cowe, was drawn with a rope to get the young Falcons from their eyrie in 1860.

The Peregrine nested at Fast Castle in 1879, and at Lumsden rocks in 1880. In 1881 it had its eyrie in the cliff at Hawksheugh, near Fast Castle; and in the following year it appears to have nested at Blakey. Mr. J. Campbell-Noble has informed me that the eyrie was at Earnsheugh in 1885. On the 22nd of April

1886, a pair of Peregrines were seen by Mr. W. Evans, Edinburgh, at Fast Castle, where they appeared to be nesting; and the young were observed there in the following June. The eyrie at Fast Castle was again occupied in the summers of 1887 and 1888.

Raven

Although this species does not now breed on the sea-coast of Berwickshire, and is but seldom seen in the county, it appears to have been comparatively common long ago; its chief resort being the precipitous cliffs in the neighbourhood of Fast Castle and St. Abb's Head, where in some crevice of the rock, at a vast height above the boiling surge below, it placed its nest and reared its young.

Ring Ouzel

Dowlaw Dean, near Fast Castle, appears to be a favourite haunt of the Ring Ouzel on its arrival in spring, as it has been often noticed there in April.

Rock Dove

Mr. Hardy writes to me that further along the coast towards the west there are several resorts of this bird about the Gull Rocks, in the neighbourhood of Fast Castle, and again at the Rammel Cove, which is nearly opposite Dowlaw Mill Pond. He adds that it likewise nests at Windylaw Cove, which is towards the Redheugh Shore, at Siccar, and in the cave mouth at Swallowcraig, and at Greenheugh, near Oldcambus.

Shag or Green Cormorant

The Green Cormorant is found on the coast of Berwickshire at all seasons of the year, and breeds at the Brander Cove, a lofty shelving ridge of rocks which runs out into the sea about a mile to the east of Fast Castle.

Woodcock

Woodcocks generally make their first appearance in autumn in the neighbourhood of the sea-coast about Lamberton, Fast Castle, and Redheugh, where they sometimes drop into hedges and turnip fields on their arrival, being exhausted by their long flight; but they soon spread inland and take up their quarters for the season in their usual haunts.

Wren

Mr. Hardy, Oldcambus, writing in 1879 upon the effects of the previous winter, mentions that in his neighbourhood the destruction amongst Wrens was very great, and that they had almost disappeared from the woods and deans. 'I saw a Wren amongst the rocks near Fast Castle, on the evening of 30th June, 1887, when I was watching the salmon-fishers drawing their nets in the sea there.'

Appendix 4

Poem by Walter Chisholm, Shepherd Lad at Redheugh Farm

[From William Cairns (ed.), *Poems by the Late Walter Chisholm* (Edinburgh, 1879)]

FAST CASTLE

I stand on the rock that, for ages on ages,
  Has braved the fierce wrath of the wild rolling tide,
The tide that below me still thunders and rages,
  All vainly, to humble its stern rugged pride.

I gaze on the ruins all crumbling and hoary,
  That often have echoed the loud battle fray;
Gone – gone is their strength and long-faded glory,
  Defaced by the finger of ruthless Decay.

How short is the day of Man's proudest creation!
  How like its creator a swift passing shade!
Like 'mist on the mountain' it fades from its station,
  And green grows the spot where its relics are laid!

As backward I look down the long dreamy vista
  Of years – that have sunk under Time's swelling wave!
Old scenes rise before me, dim, cloud-like, and misty,
  From out of the dark gloom of Oblivion's grave!

I see high above me the massive walls towering,
  Where Silence enthroned reigns supreme over all;
The battlements silent are frowning and lowering,
  And hushed is the clank of the draw-bridge's fall.

I see the steel-helmeted warriors striding,
  But rust dims their armour, unheard is each foot;
And mark! yonder boat on the blue billows riding,
  Her oars are all idle, her rowers are mute!

The ensign, that high o'er the castle is showing,
  Hangs gloomily downward in deep, darksome fold;
Untouched by the breezes that sea-ward are blowing –
  Its 'scutcheon is hidden – its motto untold.

But Twilight's dim shadows, dark, gathering o'er me,
  Dispel the illusion – ah! short was its reign!
And slowly it flits, like a ghost, from before me,
  And leaves me alone 'mid the ruins again.

Alone, with my thoughts, while the waves round me
  dashing,
  Seem wailing a dirge for the fate of my dream;
And from yon bold headland, now waning, now flashing,
  The 'Star of St. Abbs' shows his bright, warning beam.

Beam on, thou fair Beacon Light! o'er the blue ocean!
  To me thou art dearer than turret or dome,
Though surges are seething in wildest commotion,
  Thy ray guides the tempest-tossed mariner home.

Appendix 5

Maps Examined for this History of Fast Castle

DATE	AUTHOR	CASTLE NAME SHOWN ON MAP	DETAILS OF CONTENT AND PUBLICATION
1573	Abraham Ortelius	Faus castell	Map of Scotland. *Scotia Tabula*. Published in *Additamentum Theatri Orbis Terrarum* (1573). The first occasion that Scotland was included in a modern atlas.
1578	John Leslie	Fastcastel	Map of Scotland. *Scotiae regni antiquissimi accurata descripto*. Published in *De origine, moribus, et rebus gestis Scotorum* (1578).
1607	William Hole	Fast ca	Map of Scotland. *Scotia Regnum*. Published in the 1607 edition of Camden's *Brittania*.
1610	John Speed	Fast cast	Map of Great Britain. *The Kingdome of Great Britaine and Ireland*. Published in *The Theatre of the Empire of Great Britaine* (1611).
1610	John Speed	Fast-ca	Map of Scotland. *The Kingdome of Scotland*. Published as previous entry.
1640- 1650	Robert Gordon	Fast-castell	Map of Berwickshire. *A Description of the Merche*. Castle represented by small symbol. Shows Cockburnspath, Old Cambus and Coldingham. Manuscript.
1635	Willem Blaeu	Fast cast	Map of Scotland. *Scotia Regnum*. Published in *Theatrum Orbis Terrarum sive Atlas Novus* (1635).
1654	Joannis Blaeu (from Timothy Pont)	Fast castell	*Map of the Merce or Shirrefdome of Berwick*. Published in *Theatrum Orbis Terrarum sive Atlas Novus*, v (1654). Castle shown as a four-sided building with settlements or farms belonging to it. Published by W. & J. Blaeu.
1688	John Adair	False Castle	Map of the Firth of Forth from his *A True and Exact Hydrographical Description of the Sea Coasts and Islands of Scotland* (1703).

1695	Robert Morden	Fast Castel	Map of Scotland from Camden's *Britannia* (1695 edn.).
1725	Herman Moll	Fast Castle	County map of *The Shire of Berwick.* Published in *A Set of Thirty Six New and Correct Maps of Scotland* (1725). Shows Redheugh and St. Helen's Church. In A. Thomson, *Coldingham Parish and Priory* (1908).
1747–1755	General William Roy	Fast Castle	*The Military Survey of Scotland,* Sheet 9/3. Scale 1000 yards to 1 inch. In the area from Lummisden to St. Helen's Church, indicates Dowlaw Mill, Dowlaw, Oldtown, Windlaws (Windylaws), Fallowbank and Redheugh. Road from Ayton to Old Cambus depicted as complete, while road from Eyemouth via Coldingham goes through farms of Windylaws and Redheugh. Field system of runrigs well defined.
1771	Captain Armstrong & Son	Fastcastle in ruins	The *Map of the County of Berwick.* Shows farms of Lumsden, Dowlaw, Fallowbank, Windybank, Redheugh and Old Cambus. Road from Ayton through Coldingham Moor shown as a broken track.
1776	Moyston Armstrong	Fast Castle in ruins	Published in *An Actual Survey of the Great Post Roads between London and Edinburgh* (1776). As previous item, but omits Fallowbank and Windybank.
1782	Anon	Fast Castle	Map of Scotland. *A New and Correct Map of Scotland.* Published in Spencer's *History of England* (circa 1801).
1821	John Thomson	Fast Castle	Map of south-east Berwickshire. Shows farms of Lumsden, Dowlaw, Falabank, Redheugh, East Mains, West Mains and Old Cambus. Road from Ayton to Dunglass shown as complete except at Old Cambus.
1826	Sharp, Greenwood & Fowler	Fast Castle Ruins	*Map of the County of Berwick.* Shows farms of Lumsdaine, Dowlaw, Redheugh, East Mains, West Mains and Old Cambus.
1864	Ordnance Survey	Fast Castle	Scale 1 inch to 1 mile. In an area from Lumsdaine to Old

Cambus, this shows Dowlaw, Redheugh, East Mains and West Mains, together with Soldier's Dyke, and other archaeological sites.

1942..Ordnance Survey	Fast Castle (Ruins)	Sheet 11. 14. Scale 1:2500. Original survey 1856, revised 1906. Covers an area from near Lumsdaine Farm to Dowlaw Dam beside Lowries Knowes. Shows field system with acreage and Bench Mark at Fast Castle.
1978..Ordnance Survey	Fast Castle Head	Sheet NT 86:96. Eyemouth. Scale 1:25,000. Shows Lumsdaine, Dowlaw, Redheugh, Old Cambus, East and West Mains. Also shown are several sites of archaeological interest and line of Soldier's Dyke.

Appendix 6

Paintings and Drawings of Fast Castle

DATE[1]	ARTIST	DETAILS OF CONTENT AND PUBLICATION
1789	Adam de Cardonnel	A. de Cardonnel, *Picturesque Antiquities of Scotland* (1793). Engraving. Shows ruins of hall and part of brewhouse. This is the earliest portrayal of the castle known to us. Useful for analysis of keep.
1822	John Thomson[2]	Robert Napier, *John Thomson of Duddingston* (1919), and elsewhere. Painted for Sir Walter Scott and still at Abbotsford. A realistic view of the castle from the mainland.
1826	John Thomson	Sir Walter Scott, *Provincial Antiquities of Scotland* (1826). Engraving after a painting by Thomson. View of the castle from below looking west. This is a romantic painting with castle keep complete, and unrecognisable scenery.
1820s–1830s	John Thomson	Andrew Lang, *James VI and the Gowrie Mystery* (1902). View from landward side. Has some resemblance to 1822 painting, but with considerable romantic treatment. A mixture of fact and fantasy.
		Napier, *John Thomson of Duddingston.* View of castle from below looking south. Keep and castle cliff seem similar to 1826 engraving, only looking the other way. Keep again shown as complete.
1828	J. Ewbank	Robert Chambers, *The Picture of Scotland* (1828). Engraving. View from below, looking west. Is very similar in content and style to the 1826 engraving after John Thomson.
ca 1828	James Skene	James Skene, *Locations of the Waverley Novels* (1829). Engraving. View of promontory and ruins from most northerly point. Shows ruins of the keep in a very similar manner to that of Cardonnel. The earliest known portrayal of the lower half of the castle.

1829–1834	John Thomson	T. M. Richardson, *The Castles of the English and Scottish Border* (1834) and others. Fast Castle in a storm. View from below, looking south. The scenery is vaguely recognisable, but ruins shown are unintelligible.
1831	Copley Fielding	*Landscape Illustrations of the Waverley Novels* (1832). View from below, looking west. Keep similar to 1826 engraving. Also shows ship in difficulties.
1836	Alexander Carr	Carr, *A History of Coldingham Priory* (1836). Engraving. Roughly similar to Skene's engraving, showing keep in ruins. A somewhat childlike drawing.
1836	H. Melville	M. C. Pelle, *Landscape Illustrations of the Waverley Novels, by Sir Walter Scott* (n.d.) and elsewhere. Engraving. Entitled 'The Tower of Wolf's Crag', this picture is an excellent example of artistic licence. Taken from the landward side, it shows a complete tower keep amidst ruins. Obviously meant to represent Wolf's Crag from *The Bride of Lammermoor.*
1837	T. Allom	William Beattie, *Scotland Illustrated* (1838). Engraving. View from below looking west. Promontory quite recognisable, showing upper and lower levels. Keep once more shown as complete. Also shows George IV's squadron passing by on the way to Leith in 1822.
1844–1870	Mrs A. Logan Home	Major G.J.N. Logan Home, *History of the Logan Family* (1934). Watercolour. This would seem to be a copy of Thomson's painting of 1822, as its content is very similar.
1851	Clarkson Stanfield, R.A	John P. Lawson, *Scotland Delineated* (1855), ii. Entitled 'Fast Castle from the Sea', this picture, partially romantic in its treatment of the castle, gives a very vivid impression of the site. Part of the ruins of the keep seem to be based on fact, but there is much artistic licence.
1851	Clarkson Stanfield, R.A	Published in a series of 120 engravings illustrating the Abbotsford edition of the *Waverley Novels* (1851). Engraving. A view from the entrance to the castle looking towards the Bass Rock. It shows only a small portion of the causeway and entrance tower foundations.

1851 John Thomson	Published as above. Engraving. This engraving after Thomson's 1822 painting is almost identical to the original.
1852 Blacklock	W. H. Maxwell, *Border Tales and Legends of the Cheviots and Lammermuir* (1852). Engraving. Similar treatment to 1826 engraving after Thomson's painting. Keep shown as complete.
1859 William Bartlett	James Taylor, *Pictorial History of Scotland* (1859). Engraving. Frontal view of the castle taken from the entrance. Although some artistic licence has been used in this drawing, it is a fairly realistic view, probably showing the ruins much as they were about this time.
1863 Artist not known	Adam and Charles Black, *Picturesque Tourist of Scotland* (1863). Engraving. View of promontory and castle from most northerly point. Although the lower half of the promontory has some basis in fact, it is obvious that this artist has produced a composite picture from several previous works. The keep is shown entire, but is largely imaginative.
1857– Sam Bough, 1878 R.S.A.	Published in an edition of *The Bride of Lammermoor.* Engraving. Entitled 'Wolf's Crag', this engraving is pure fantasy. It shows the castle at the end of a promontory, but it is quite unrecognisable as Fast Castle.
1889 James Hardy?	David MacGibbon and Thomas Ross, *Castellated and Domestic Architecture of Scotland* (1889). Engraving. Rough plan of the promontory showing some of the existing walls and foundations. Also a rough sketch of the castle and promontory from below looking west. The ruins are quite unrecognisable. It includes an inset sketch of the existing keep aumbry or cupboard. The plan and two sketches are possibly by James Hardy of Old Cambus, and are certainly not of MacGibbon and Ross's usual quality.
1977 K. R. Murdoch and J. Field	Edinburgh Archaeological Field Society, *Fast Castle* (1977). Initial conjectural reconstruction of the castle, as viewed from the entrance way. Based on the 1859 engraving by Bartlett.
1986 David Simon	This publication.

1. Where the date of an artist's work and publication coincide, it is not implied that the illustration was necessarily produced in that year.
2. The most complete descriptive list of John Thomson's paintings of Fast Castle can be found in Robert Napier's biography of the artist. Napier lists 20 paintings, including their owners, as well as information on when some of them were exhibited.

Appendix 7

Photographs of Fast Castle

DATE PHOTOGRAPHER	DETAILS OF CONTENT AND PUBLICATION
1902 J. Valentine (ca.) & Sons, Dundee	View from the mainland, near entrance. Very similar to the present, except that path into castle is loose rubble. Also general view of promontory from the east. Both in Andrew Lang, *James VI and the Gowrie Mystery* (1902).
1908 William M. (ca.) Sandison	General view of promontory from the sea in front of the 'Castle Hole'. Also general view of castle ruins taken from Hawksheugh. Both in A. Thomson, *Coldingham Parish and Priory* (1908).
1908 William Douglas	Two views, very similar to those of 1902 listed above. *Proceedings of the Society of Antiquaries of Scotland,* lv (1920-1).
1933 Scottish Mountaineering Club	Entrance to 'Chapel Cave' under the end point of the promontory with climber on the cave face.
1946 National Aerial Survey	Aerial view of Dowlaw Farm and Fast Castle. Sheet Nos. 7910 and 7911.
1961 Royal Commission on the Ancient and Historical Monuments of Scotland	Set of views of castle, including one of the aumbry or cupboard in the keep wall which has since been destroyed.
1979 Prof. Dennis Harding	Set of aerial views. Available at RCAHMS.
1980 RCAHMS	Set of aerial views.
1971- Edinburgh 1986 Archaeological Field Society	Mainly colour prints and slides of excavations at Fast Castle.

Appendix 8

Project 'Jock Trap': Survey of the Fast Castle Caves, June 1976. 'Results, Findings & Conclusions'

By the late Lieut. Adrian Ashby-Smith

The project team was required to investigate two known tunnel entrances at the base of Fast Castle promontory, and to verify the existence (or otherwise) of suspected passage entries in the cliff faces of the foundation.

One cave was previously explored (although not in detail) in 1920 and in 1969. This cave is shown as 'No. 2' on the attached plan [not illustrated]. Cave No. 1 was first entered by members of the 16 Bn expedition. Measurement revealed that the cave extended for 91' into the cliff beneath the castle, but actually ran and terminated outside the area bounded by the walls of the castle, 100' above. It was established that there were no alternative means of exit from the cave.

Cave No. 2 had previously been explored to an estimated depth of 80 yards. Measurements taken indicate that tide-swept boulders have been packed to the back of the cave roof level (conjectural vertical height: 18') from a distance of 260' from the cave mouth. Removal of flotsam revealed a passage over the bank of spoil. This was originally too narrow for exploration, although its visible length was 20'. This was dug out to a depth of 3' and extended physically to a length of 25'. At the conclusion of the project, a number of animal bones had been located in the soil at the furthest reach of the passage, and a further air passage – giving another 10' visibility – had been located. Time prevented exploitation of what could prove to be an exciting extension to the passage.

A number of interesting factors have come out of the work done by the expedition:-

a. The tunnel beneath the castle has been penetrated to a greater depth than ever before.

b. The presence of bones in clay soil indicates that there actually is (or was) a passage of connection between surface and tunnel (a vertical distance of approximately 120'). It is hoped that examination of the bones by the Edinburgh Museum* will verify the validity of this conjecture.

c. Members of the Archaeological Society have thought in terms of the tunnel connecting with a known well, which has been dug on the landward side of the castle entrance. Measurements now available indicate that this may not be the case, but that there may be a form of shaft some 30 metres north of the well beneath a visible ground depression. Without more exact evidence (i.e. further exploration of the cave passage) however, the possibility of a horizontal passage – possibly man-made – from well to cave cannot be ruled out. The suggestion of such a passage being man-made is put forward because any such connection would be constructed across the rock strata – and there is no evidence of that form of fault exploitation in the area examined.

d. The possibility of entering the castle from Cave No. 1 has been ruled out by exploration made by members of the project team. Direction and length of cave serve to support this statement. Additionally, the floor of this cave is above the level of normal high tide and the rock outcrop which shields this portion of the cliff from the sea would render foot access from ships virtually impossible.

e. High tide at Cave 2 would permit entry to the tunnel, facilitated by longboat. The rocks around the cave entrance have formed a perfect natural harbour (at low and high tides) there. Access at low tide to the cave is without problem, from the cove area. Access to the castle, by scaling the cliff, is difficult (at this time) but not impossible. The bucket and crane (as shown on the 1549 plan) would stand directly above a rock ledge at the harbour side.

f. There is no evidence to substantiate the existence of passages or tunnels connecting Cave No. 2 to the south-eastern face of the promontory. Observations made – prior to the digging-out of the main cave passage – gave no indication of air movement within the cave.

The project undertaken has proved to be of immeasurable interest to all participants – the physical exertion involved has succeeded in reducing the waist measurements of all. Climbing and caving abilities have been established, with the enthusiasm for more of the same type of activity. It is hoped that the results obtained have been of use to the Edinburgh Archaeologists. Working with those specialists has been absorbing, amusing, and instructive.

* Royal Museum of Scotland, Chambers Street

[A personalised account of the 'Jock Trap' exercise was written by the late Lieut. Ashby-Smith, and is available from the Edinburgh Archaeological Field Society.]

Notes

Introduction

1. Mark Napier, *Memoirs of John Napier of Merchiston* (Edinburgh, 1834), p. 221. Facsimile illustration in *The National Manuscripts of Scotland,* (Edinburgh, 1871), iii.
2. William Douglas, 'Fast Castle and its Owners: Some Notes on Their History', *Proc. Soc. of Antiquaries of Scotland,* lv (1920-21), 56-83.
3. Ibid., p. 78.
4. Fred Douglas, *Gold at Wolf's Crag* (Edinburgh, 1971). In 1970 Kathleen Fidler published a children's story, *The Gold of Fast Castle* (London, 1970).
5. Andrew Thomson, *Coldingham Parish and Priory* (Galashiels, 1908).
6. *Proceedings of the Berwickshire Naturalists' Club,* xx (1906-8).
7. Hall of Dunglass Muniments, Scottish Record Office, GD 206.
8. Fuller justification for this assertion will be given in the Society's forthcoming publication on the castle's early history. The rest of this Introduction is mainly adapted from Douglas, 'Fast Castle and Its Owners', and Edinburgh Archaeological Field Society, *Fast Castle* (Edinburgh, 1977).
9. It is hoped to cover the sale of these lands, including the history of Robert Logan's estate, from his death until his posthumous forfeiture in 1609, in a future publication.

Chapter 1. Logan, Douglas, the Earl of Dunbar, and Arnott

1. John Shearer, *Old Maps and Map Makers of Scotland* (Stirling, 1905) includes a reproduction of Abraham Ortelius's map of Scotland. Shearer states that Scotland's first printed map was published in 1570. In fact it appeared in 1573, the 1570 map being one of Great Britain: Royal Scottish Geographical Society, *The Early Maps of Scotland* (Edinburgh, 1936).
2. Ibid..
3. John Speed, *Maps of Great Britain and Scotland* (1610). See also Appendix 5.
4. IVth International Conference on the History of Cartography, *The Mapping of Scotland* (Edinburgh, 1971), p. 9.
5. Angus Graham, 'Archaeology on a Great Post Road', *Proceedings of the Society of Antiquaries of Scotland,* xcvi (1962-3), 322-3.
6. Daniel Defoe, *A Tour Through the Whole Island of Great Britain* (2 vols., [first published 1724-6], Everyman edition, London, 1962), ii, 284.
7. G. J. N. Logan Home, *History of the Logan Family* (Edinburgh, 1934), pp. 80-2.
8. *Register of the Great Seal of Scotland* (11 vols., Edinburgh, 1882-1914), vi, 1593-1608, 602-3, No. 1663. *History of the Berwickshire Naturalists' Club,* xx (1906-8), 97, states: 'On 10th August 1605 Robert Logan of Restalrig obtained a Charter of the lands of Wester Lumsden after a sale of the teinds by Logan

of date 10th November 1602 to Archibald Douglas of Pittendreich.'

9. Thomson, *Coldingham Parish and Priory*, p. 248.

10. Sir James Balfour Paul (ed.), *The Scots Peerage* (9 vols., Edinburgh, 1904–14), vi, 362–4; William Fraser, *The Douglas Book* (Edinburgh,1885), p. 321.

11. John Anderson (ed.), *Calendar of the Laing Charters* (Edinburgh, 1899), p. 365, No. 1497.

12. For an explanation of the legal term 'superiority', see the Glossary.

13. Historical Manuscripts Commission, *Report on the Manuscripts of Colonel David Milne Home* (London, 1902), p. 233.

14. William Anderson, *The Scottish Nation*, (3 vols., Edinburgh, 1863), ii, 75.

15. Paul (ed.), *Scots Peerage*, iii, 286–9.

16. Sir James Balfour, *Historical Works* (4 vols., Edinburgh, 1824–5), ii, 16–17.

17. Leslie Stephen (ed.), *Dictionary of National Biography* (London, 1885–), 'George Home'. Anderson, *Scottish Nation*, ii, 75, states that it was the Earl of Mar who accompanied the Earl of Dunbar to Scotland in 1606.

18. Anderson, *Scottish Nation*, ii, 75.

19. Historical Manuscripts Commission, *Report on the Manuscripts of the Family of Home of Renton* (London, 1876), p. 648; *Register of the Great Seal*, vi, 646–7, No. 1773.

20. *The Acts of the Parliaments of Scotland* (12 vols., London, 1814–75), iv, 292–7.

21. *Dictionary of National Biography* gives his date of death as 30 January.

22. Paul (ed.), *Scots Peerage*, iii, 286–8.

23. *Register of the Great Seal*, vii, 259, No. 699.

24. Thomson, *Coldingham Parish and Priory*, p. 254, quoting Anderson (ed.), *Calendar of the Laing Charters*, No. 1906.

25. Ibid, p. 255.

26. Thomson, *Coldingham Parish and Priory*, p. 248; Paul (ed.), *Scots Peerage*, iv, 475.

27. *Register of the Great Seal 1609–1620*, vii, 349–50, No. 963.

28. Paul (ed.), *Scots Peerage*, iii, 504–6. For a fuller acount of Sir Gideon Murray, see 'Sir Gideon Murray of Elibank', *The Border Magazine*, x, No. 110 (1905), 46–8.

29. *Register of the Great Seal*, vii, 657, No. 1812.

30. Paul (ed.), *Scots Peerage*, iii, 504–6.

31. *Register of the Great Seal*, vii, 521–2, No. 1428.

32. Eric Rankin, *Cockburnspath* (Edinburgh, 1981), p. 8.

33. *The Lord Provosts of Edinburgh 1296–1932* (Edinburgh, 1932), p. 30.

34. John Brown Craven, *Sir John Arnot of Barswick and the Family of Arnot in South Ronaldshay*, (Kirkwall, 1913), p. 7.

35. Ibid., p. 6.

36. *Acts of the Parliaments of Scotland*, iv, 293.

37. Historical Manuscripts Commission, *Report on the Manuscripts of the Earl of Marchmont* (London, 1894), p. 79, No. 47.

38. Craven, *Family of Arnot*, p. 8.

39. *Acts of the Parliaments of Scotland* iv, 448–9.

40. James Arnott, *The House of Arnot and Some of its Branches: a Family History* (Edinburgh, 1918), p. 66.

41. Ibid., pp. 63-4.
42. Arnott, *House of Arnot*, p. 95.
43. Ibid., p. 96.
44. Hall of Dunglass Muniments, Scottish Record Office, GD 206 1/13.
45. Ibid., GD 206 1/14.
46. Rankin, *Cockburnspath*, p. 9. There seems to be some confusion about this particular William Arnott. Rankin states that he was the second son of William Arnott and Mariote Wallace, and a brother of John Arnott, burgess of Edinburgh. According to Arnott, *House of Arnot*, he was the second son of Sir John Arnott of Berswick. Other evidence would seem to support this view.
47. Arnott, *House of Arnot*, p. 91; Rankin, *Cockburnspath*, p. 10; Hall of Dunglass Muniments, GD 206 1/22, 24, 29.
48. *Register of the Privy Council of Scotland*, 1st Ser., 1545-1625 (14 vols., Edinburgh, 1877-98), xiii, 539.
49. Carr, *Coldingham Priory*, p. 92; Hall of Dunglass Muniments, GD 206 2/174, f. 2.
50. *Register of the Great Seal*, viii, 13, No. 40.

Chapter 2. The Homes and the Stewarts

1. Historical Manuscripts Commission, *Report on the Manuscripts of the Duke of Athole and the Earl of Home* (London, 1891), p. 184.
2. *Acts of the Parliaments of Scotland*, iv, 360-1. See also *Register of the Great Seal*, vii, 106-9, concerning the 1610 grant.
3. Paul (ed.), *Scots Peerage*, iv, 463-5. See also the previous reference to James Home of Whiterig and his wife Anne Home in the same volume.
4. Ibid., ii, 168-73.
5. *Memorial for Sir John Home of Manderston anent his claim upon the Estate of Coldingham* (Edinburgh, 1749), p. 1. In this work it is stated that Francis Stuart, Earl of Bothwell, was forfeited in 1592. This forfeiture was caused by the earl committing the treasonable offence of breaking into the palace of Holyrood with a drawn sword, and attempting to seize Chancellor Maitland.
6. *Letters and State Papers during the reign of King James VI* (Edinburgh, 1838), pp. 324-8.
7. *Melros Papers, or State Papers and Miscellaneous Correspondence of Thomas Earl of Melros* (Edinburgh, 1837), pp. 370-2.
8. Historical Manuscripts Commission, *Colonel David Milne Home*, pp. 198-9, No. 432.
9. *Acts of the Parliaments of Scotland*, iv, 657-60. *Register of the Great Seal*, viii, 78-9, No. 232.
10. Ibid., No. 231; Thomson, *Coldingham Parish and Priory*, p. 248.
11. *Register of the Privy Council*, 1st Ser., xii, 679-80.
12. Ibid., 2nd Ser., iv, 664.
13. Ibid., p. 16.
14. Historical Manuscripts Commission, *Colonel David Milne Home*, pp. 203-4.
15. *Register of the Great Seal*, viii, 166-7, No. 479.
16. Anderson (ed.), *Calendar of the Laing Charters*, p. 476, No. 1985.

17. *Register of the Privy Council*, 2nd Ser., iv, 160.
18. Ibid., iv, 641.
19. *Inquisitionum Retornatarum Abbreviatio*, i, Berwick, No. 174; ii, Berwick, No. 533.
20. *Acts of the Parliaments of Scotland*, vi, Part 1, 193.
21. Ibid., p. 534.
22. Historical Manuscripts Commission, *Colonel David Milne Home*, pp. 202–4, No. 439.
23. Ibid., p. 204, No. 440.

Chapter 3. The Hepburns and Ramsays

1. Historical Manuscripts Commission, *Duke of Athole and Earl of Home*, p. 109.
2. Paul (ed.), *Scots Peerage*, iv, 466–7.
3. Ibid., p. 477.
4. Earl of Stirling, *Register of Royal Letters* (Edinburgh, 1885), p. 847.
5. Anderson (ed.), *Calendar of the Laing Charters*, p. 540, No.2282. According to Thomson, *Coldingham Parish and Priory*, 'On 12th July [1622], James, Earl of Home, granted the life-rent to his wife, Jean Douglas, daughter of William, Earl of Morton, of the Lands and Barony of Dunglass, Auldcambus, and Fast Castle.' He cites as his authority *Laing Charters*, No. 1039. Thomson seems to have become completely mixed up here. It must be assumed that he is referring to James, second Earl of Home; however, it was James, the third Earl, who was married to Jean Douglas. The event to which Thomson apparently alludes occurred in 1640, and can be found in *Laing Charters*, No. 2282. No. 1039 has no connection with Fast Castle.
6. *Inquisitionum Retornatarum Abbreviatio*, i, Berwick, No.238.
7. Hall of Dunglass Muniments, GD 206 2/174/3.
8. *Register of the Great Seal*, 1634–51, pp. 383–4, No. 1039.
9. Ibid., 387, No. 1050.
10. Ibid., p. 425, No. 1134.
11. Hall of Dunglass Muniments, GD 206 2/174/3.
12. *Register of the Great Seal*, 1634–51, p. 454, No. 1215.
13. Ibid.; James Duncan, *The Descent of the Hepburns of Monkrig* (Edinburgh, 1911), p. 43.
14. Ibid., p. 42.
15. Rankin, *Cockburnspath*, p. 58.
16. *Register of the Great Seal*, 1634–50, pp. 465–6, No. 1240.
17. Carr, *Coldingham Priory*, p. 92. Carr, the earliest source of this information, states that Sir Patrick was dispossessed by Alexander, Earl of Home. In 1644 James, the third earl, still held the title. He died in 1666. No corroboration for Carr's statement has been found.
18. *Register of the Great Seal*, 1634–50, pp. 641–2, No. 1702.
19. Thomson, *Coldingham Parish and Priory*, p. 249. Both *History of the Berwickshire Naturalists' Club*, xx (1906–8) and Thomson, *Coldingham Parish and Priory*, state that 'on 5 August, *1647* John Hepburn, heir apparent of Wauchton, and Marie Ross, his wife, got a Charter of Novodamus of the Lands which his father, Sir Patrick Hepburn held.'

20. *Register of the Privy Council*, 2nd Ser., i, 185–99.
21. Ibid., p. 627.
22. William Camden, *Britannia* (London, 1607 edn.), pp. 686–7.
23. William Camden, *Britannia* (London, 1610 edn.), pp. 10–11.
24. William Camden, *Britannia* (London, 1695 edn.), p. 895.
25. John Monniepennie, *An Abridgement or Summarie of the Scots Chronicles* (Edinburgh, 1612), pp. 74–5.
26. Douglas, 'Fast Castle and its Owners', p. 60.
27. *A Large Relation of the Fight at Leith Neere Edenburgh* (Edinburgh, 1650), pp. 1–2.
28. *Mercurius Politicus*, Thursday, 6–13 Feb 1651 [Brit. Lib. E 623 (14)].
29. Ibid., No. 39, Thursday, 27 February to 6 March [Brit. Lib. E 626 (15)].
30. *The Weekly Intelligencer of the Commonwealth*, No. 11, p. 85, Tuesday, 4 March to Tuesday 11 March 1650 (1651) [Brit. Lib. E 626 (2)].
31. Ibid., p. 86.
32. Hugo Arnot, *The History of Edinburgh* (Edinburgh, 1816), pp. 414–5.
33. Rankin, *Cockburnspath*, p. 56, from Nicolson Papers 1623–86, Scottish Record Office, RH 15/97/1–8.
34. *Register of the Great Seal*, x, 1652–9, 185–6, No. 425.
35. Ibid., pp. 186–7, No. 428.
36. Ibid., p. 188, No. 434.
37. Ibid., pp. 188–9, No. 435.
38. James J. Grant, *Edinburgh Register of Testaments* (Edinburgh, 1898). Duncan, *Descent of the Hepburns of Monkrig*, p. 44, states that John Hepburn died before 1667.
39. *Register of the Privy Council*, 3rd Ser., iii, 143.
40. Scottish Record Office, Index to the General Register of Sasines, 1660–70. Several writers make the mistake of saying that it was Sir Andrew, senior, of Abbotshall who married Margaret Hepburn.
41. Some authors state that it was Sir Andrew Ramsay, senior, who was created a baronet. Millar, *Fife*, p. 119, states that Sir Andrew Ramsay, junior, was created a baronet on 23 January 1669.
42. Hall of Dunglass Muniments, GD 206 2/174/6.
43. Ibid., GD 206 2/174/7.
44. Several authors confuse Sir Andrew Ramsay of Waughton's date of death with that of his father and vice-versa. Sir Andrew Ramsay of Abbotshall seems to have died on 17 January 1688. Other writers state that he died in 1709 without issue, apparently confusing him with his grandson, the third baronet.
45. *Inquisitionum Retornatarum Abbreviatio*, Berwick Retours, No. 402; Fife Retours, No. 1187; Haddington Retours, No. 338.
46. Hall of Dunglass Muniments, GD 206 2/174/7.
47. Loc. cit..
48. Loc. cit.. Sources of information on the Ramsays of Abbotshall and Waughton include, Scottish Record Office, Indices to the General Register of Sasines, and Indices to the Register of Deeds; Stephen (ed.), *Dictionary of National Biography*, xlvii, 235–6; G. E. C[okayne] (ed.), *Complete Baronetage* (5 vols., London, 1900–6), iv, 273; Millar, *Fife*, pp. 118–19; Paul (ed.), *Scots Peerage*, iii, 452; Anderson, *Scots Nation*, iii, 323.

Chapter 4. The Halls of Dunglass

1. C[okayne] (ed.), *Complete Baronetage*, iv, 353.
2. Hall of Dunglass Muniments, GD 206 2/1. C[okayne] (ed.), *Complete Baronetage*, states that Sir John Hall married first Catherine, widow of John Mein, and secondly Margaret, daughter of George Fleming of Kilconquhar.
3. *Acts of the Parliaments of Scotland*, ix, 503-6.
4. Ibid., p. 505; *Extracts from the Records of the Burgh of Edinburgh 1689-1701* (Edinburgh,1885), p. 196. Rankin, *Cockburnspath*, p. 82, states that Sir John Hall bought Cockburnspath in 1693. This presumably would be the original date of sale.
5. *Lord Provosts of Edinburgh*, p. 55.
6. Rankin, *Cockburnspath*, p. 83.
7. *Acts of the Parliaments of Scotland*, ix, 503-6.
8. Hall of Dunglass Muniments, GD 206 No.57.
9. Ibid., GD 206 2/1.
10. Rankin, *Cockburnspath*, p. 83.
11. C[okayne] (ed.), *Complete Baronetage*, iv, 353-4; Hall of Dunglass Muniments, GD 206 2/1.
12. This publication is not intended to explore the history of the Hall family and Dunglass estate in any depth. It is obvious, however, that a comprehensive study of the abundant manuscript material available at the Scottish Record Office would generously repay the effort involved and greatly advance knowledge of the area.
13. Rankin, *Cockburnspath*, p. 52.
14. Ibid., p. 2.
15. *Polwarth Manuscripts*, v, 1725-80, No. 56, Sir James Hall to the Earl of Marchmont.
16. Hall of Dunglass Muniments, GD 206 No. 237.
17. C[okayne] (ed.), *Complete Baronetage*, iv, 353-4. Hall of Dunglass Muniments, GD 206 4/19.
18. Scottish Record Office, 1863, Service of Heirs, i, 1740-49.
19. J. R. Ward and K. L. Mitchell, 'The Barony of Dowlaw, Berwickshire Farming in the Eighteenth Century' (Edinburgh Archaeological Field Society, 1978).
20. Alexander Fenton, *Scottish Country Life* (Edinburgh, 1976), p. 11.
21. See Appendix 2(b)-(c).
22. Robert Kerr, *General View of the Agriculture of the County of Berwick* (London, 1809), pp. 92, 118.
23. *Scottish Genealogist*, xx, No. 3, 72.
24. Loc. cit..
25. Rev. Thomas Thomson (ed.), *Biographical Dictionary of Eminent Scotsmen* (3 vols., London, 1868-70), ii, 201-3.
26. *New Statistical Account of Scotland: Berwickshire* (Edinburgh, 1841), pp. 311-2.
27. Rankin, *Cockburnspath*, p. 48.
28. Hall of Dunglass Muniments, GD 206 5/16.
29. *History of the Berwickshire Naturalists' Club* (1856-62), 39.
30. Thomson (ed.), *Biographical Dictionary of Eminent Scotsmen*, ii, 202.
31. *New Statistical Account of Scotland: Berwickshire*, p. 310.

32. Rankin, *Cockburnspath*, pp. 86-7.
33. For the division of Coldingham Common, see Thomson, *Coldingham Parish and Priory*, pp. 51-61; *History of the Berwickshire Naturalists' Club*, xlii (1983), 109-18.
34. Rankin, *Cockburnspath*, p. 87.
35. Scottish Record Office, Service of Heirs, iv, 1830-39.
36. Ibid., v, 1860-69; 2nd Ser., vi, 1910-19.
37. *Debrett's Handbook* (London, 1985 edn.), p. 841.

Chapter 5. Fast Castle as an Antiquity

1. John Adair, *Description of the Sea-coast and Islands of Scotland* (1703).
2. *History of the Berwickshire Naturalists' Club* (1896-8), 160.
3. Stephen (ed.), *Dictionary of National Biography*, x, 41-2.
4. Sir Paul Harvey, *The Oxford Companion to English Literature* (Oxford, 1944), p. 107.
5. 'Introduction' to *The Bride of Lammermoor*, in the *Waverley Novels*, xiii (Edinburgh, 1830), 254-5.
6. Robert W. Napier, *John Thomson of Duddingston* (Edinburgh, 1919), p. 296.
7. John Gibson Lockhart, *The Life of Sir Walter Scott* (10 vols., Edinburgh, 1902), vii, 105.
8. Sir Walter Scott, *The Provincial Antiquities of Scotland* (2 vols., London, 1826), ii, 188.
9. David MacGibbon and Thomas Ross, *The Castellated and Domestic Architecture of Scotland* (5 vols., Edinburgh, 1887-92), iii, 222-3.
10. Douglas, 'Fast Castle and Its Owners', states that 'in 1880, McGibbon and Ross made some drawings of the castle and these show that much of the building has disappeared since then.' The drawings referred to indicate that only a small portion of the north-east wall of the keep had disappeared.
11. T. M. Richardson, *The Castles of the English and Scottish Border* (Newcastle upon Tyne, 1834), Part 1.
12. Robert Chambers, *The Picture of Scotland* (2 vols., Edinburgh, 1828), i, 53.
13. George Muirhead, *The Birds of Berwickshire* (2 vols., Edinburgh, 1895), ii, 1.
14. Ibid., 2-3.
15. A. G. Long, 'Extracts from the Correspondence of James Hardy', *A History of the Berwickshire Naturalists' Club*, xxxviii, Part 2 (1969), 164. However, despite Hardy's categorical statement, it seems rather doubtful whether a lightning strike could have had as much effect as he implies. Probably storm force winds were the main cause of damage.
16. William Cairns (ed.), *Poems by the Late Walter Chisholm* (Edinburgh, 1879), Preface, pp. x-xii.
17. *Scottish Mountaineering Club Journal*, xx (1933-5), 1-2.
18. Ibid., xv (1918-20), 305-9.
19. Carr, *History of Coldingham Priory*, p. 95.
20. It seems unlikely that Sang and Raeburn could have thoroughly examined the whole cave with the aid of only one candle.
21. William Douglas, 'The Exploration of the Historic Cave at Fast

Castle'; *Scottish Mountaineering Club Journal,* xv (1918–20), 305–9.

22. *A History of the Berwickshire Naturalists' Club,* xxv, 186–9.
23. Ian Campbell, 'Fast Castle', *Scottish Mountaineering Club Journal,* xx (1933–5), 102–5.
24. H. Drummond Gauld, *Brave Borderland* (London, 1935), p. 62.
25. Douglas, *Gold at Wolf's Crag,* pp. 1–5.

Chapter 6. Excavations at Fast Castle, 1971–86

1. K. R. Murdoch (ed.), 'Newsletter' of the Edinburgh Archaeological Field Society, Issue 9, May 1976, p. 1.
2. Ibid., Issue 25, May 1979, p. 2.
3. We are indebted to Nicholas Holmes and David Caldwell for analysis of the coins, to Dennis Gallagher for studying the pipe fragments, and to Trevor Cowie for identifying the Iron Age pottery found near the castle well shaft.
4. Adrian Ashby-Smith, '"Jock Trap" Expedition Report' (1976), typescript held by the Edinburgh Archaeological Field Society.
5. *The Scotsman,* 18 August 1976. Various sources give differing heights for Sangay.
6. Ibid..
7. *Edinburgh Evening News,* 17 August 1976. The story of the Sangay expedition is told by Richard Snailham, *Sangay Survived* (London, 1978).
8. Royal Commission on the Ancient and Historical Monuments of Scotland, 54 Melville Street, Edinburgh, negative nos. BWD 31/2.
9. Edinburgh Archaeological Field Society 'Newsletter', Issue 13, February 1977, pp. 3–4.
10. Dennis Harding; available at Royal Commission on the Ancient and Historical Monuments of Scotland.
11. Royal Commission on the Ancient and Historical Monuments of Scotland, negative nos. BWD 3057–60. These photographs have no connection with the Edinburgh Archaeological Field Society.
12. Although imperial units of measurement have been used so far in this *History,* metric measurements are reported for our excavations, following modern archaeological practice.
13. It is intended to produce a full archaeological report on the excavation of the lower courtyard as soon as circumstances permit.
14. Edinburgh Archaeological Field Society, 'Annual Report, 1985', Chairman's Report by K. R. Murdoch, p. 2.
15. John Wilson died in 1835, at the age of 31, just as his weekly *Tales* were becoming popular. His brother James, who continued the publication for a short time, rode to Berwickshire to enlist the help of Alexander Carr in the production of the next issue in the series. This resulted in the story, 'Coldingham Abbey or the Double Revenge'. In 1840, an Edinburgh bookseller published the first edition of the complete series, which was continued by many other contributors. We have not been able to trace original copies of the 1835 series, or a complete version of the 1840 edition, and therefore are not in a position to say when 'The Fatal Secret' was written. We have only found the story in some of the later editions, which sequentially place it

a few numbers after Carr's narrative, suggesting that it was written in 1835. As editions which contain the story do not name individual authors, we are at a loss as to who wrote it. Perhaps Carr himself was responsible.

16. John McKay Wilson and others (eds.), *Tales of the Border* (London, c. 1890), ii, 22-3.
17. It has been suggested that water supplies were also obtained by means of a natural spring emanating from the sea floor at the base of the promontory, not far from the main cave.

Glossary

Candlemas 2 February. Feast day of the Purification of the Virgin Mary, and a Scottish term day [see Martinmas].

Charter of Novodamus A charter which contains new clauses or stipulations relating to heritable property. It was and still may be used to create alterations or amend incorrect information in previous charters or title deeds.

Commendator The nominal title given to a lay abbot who held a benefice or church living. This appointment was frequently for life, and often did not require any active function to be performed.

Corslettis Corslet. A protective body cover for the chest made of leather or steel which was used by combatants in battle.

Curtain (Wall) In castle architecture, a wall which encloses a courtyard.

Denounce as a Rebel The result of failing to comply with a command of the king or his authorities after due warning. The offender was then denounced or outlawed upon three blasts of a horn given at the chief burgh where he resided, or at the market cross of Edinburgh. Debtors who failed to pay their creditors also underwent this procedure.

Heirs, Service of The legal process of entering an heir into the possession of heritable property.

Hind A farm servant occupying a farm cottage.

Hird Herdsman. A farm worker who looked after cattle or sheep.

Husbandman An old term for a working farmer.

Infeftment The old Scots legal custom of symbolically investing the owner of heritable property into his land. This indicated that the title had been completed.

Jakkis Jack. A coat, usually made of leather, which was worn in battle.

Lammas 1 August. A Scottish term day [see Martinmas].

Lang Hagbuttes Hackbut. A type of handgun used during the sixteenth and seventeenth centuries.

Leading The transport of a laden horse-drawn cart containing hay, crops, or other material. In common use at harvest time.

Maiden Scottish instrument of execution similar to the French guillotine. In Edinburgh it claimed the lives of several historic figures between 1564 and 1710, and can be viewed in the Royal Museum of Scotland, Queen Street.

Merk A Scottish silver coin equivalent to 13s 4d sterling.

Martinmas 11 November. Feast day of St. Martin, and a Scottish term day. The fourth term of the year, when rent or interest was payable, leases entered into, and workers hired.

Net Stob A stake or post used to support nets for enclosing sheep.

Pairing As in paring and burning. Old method of treating land to produce successive crops without rotation. The turf was stripped and then burnt prior to sowing. The practice tended to exhaust the soil and was superseded by more productive methods in the nineteenth century.

Pilgrim's Badge A medieval religious souvenir, made of lead or pewter. It would be bought at a shrine and normally be worn on the pilgrim's hat.

Ranging Pole Normally a one or two metre wooden pole, painted red and white. Used in archaeology for survey purposes, or to act as a scale for site photographs.

Resignation Part of the old legal process by which a vassal could be released from his heritable rights. This was accomplished by making use of a legal instrument which gave the property back to the vassal's superior.

Sasine Similar to infeftment. A symbolic investiture or seising into feudal property, by the giving of earth and stone. In the early seventeenth century a law was enacted requiring land purchases to be recorded in the Register of Sasines in Edinburgh.

Superiority The rights of ownership held by a superior of heritable property, and to whom feu duties are payable by the vassal.

Tack Lease. The landowner and his tenant would enter into a contract which stipulated the length of the tenancy and the amount of rent payable, along with other conditions.

Teind Tithe. The tenth of the produce from land. Up to the Reformation it was used for the maintenance of the clergy. Later it was due to whoever owned the right to receive payment.

Teind Sheaves Sheaves of grain due as payment of teind (q.v.) at harvest time.

Translation In church usage, the act of transferring a minister from one congregation to another.

Bibliography

Manuscripts

Scottish Record Office, Edinburgh

Hall of Dunglass Muniments (GD 206).
Indices to the General Register of Sasines.
Indices to the Register of Deeds.
Service of Heirs.

Maps, Paintings, Drawings, and Photographs

See Appendices 5-7.

Newspapers

Edinburgh Evening News.
Mercurius Politicus [British Library E 623 (14), E 626 (15)].
The Scotsman.
The Weekly Intelligencer of the Commonwealth
  [British Library E 626 (2)].

Other Printed Works

The Acts of the Parliaments of Scotland, 1124-1707 (12 vols.,
  London, 1814-75).
Adair, John, *A True and Exact Hydrographical Description of the
  Sea Coasts and Islands of Scotland* (Edinburgh, 1703).
Anderson, John (ed.), *Calendar of the Laing Charters* (Edinburgh,
  1899).
Anderson, William, *The Scottish Nation* (3 vols., Edinburgh, 1863).
Anon., *Extracts from the Records of the Burgh of Edinburgh 1689-
  1701* (Edinburgh, 1885).
_____, *A Large Relation of the Fight at Leith neer Edinburgh*
  (London, 1650).
_____, *Letters and State Papers During the Reign of King James VI*
  (Edinburgh, 1838).
_____, *The Lord Provosts of Edinburgh, 1296-1932* (Edinburgh, 1932).
_____, *Memorial for Sir John Home of Manderston anent his Claim upon
  the Estate of Coldingham* (Edinburgh, 1749).
_____, *The National Manuscripts of Scotland* (Edinburgh, 1871).
_____, 'Sir Gideon Murray of Elibank', *The Border Magazine*, x,
  No. 110 (1905), 46-8.
Arnot, Hugo, *The History of Edinburgh* (Edinburgh, 1816).

Arnott, Sir James, *The House of Arnot and Some of its Branches: a Family History* (Edinburgh, 1918).

Bain, Joseph (ed.), *The Hamilton Papers* (2 vols., Edinburgh, 1890–2).

Balfour, Sir James, *Historical Works* (4 vols., Edinburgh, 1824–5).

Beattie, William, *Scotland Illustrated* (London, 1838).

Black, Adam and Charles, *Picturesque Tourist of Scotland* (Edinburgh, 1863).

Cairns, William (ed.), *Poems by the Late Walter Chisholm* (Edinburgh, 1879).

Camden, William, *Britannia* (London, 1607, 1610, and 1695 editions).

Campbell, Ian, 'Fast Castle', *Scottish Mountaineering Club Journal* xx (1933–5).

Cardonnel, Adam de, *Picturesque Antiquities of Scotland* (London, 1793).

Carr, Alexander, *A History of Coldingham Priory* (Edinburgh, 1836).

Chambers, Robert, *The Picture of Scotland* (2 vols., Edinburgh, 1827).

C[okayne], G. E. (ed.), *Complete Baronetage* (5 vols., London, 1900–6).

Craven, John Brown, *Sir John Arnot of Barswick and the Family of Arnot in South Ronaldshay* (Kirkwall, 1913).

Debrett's Handbook (London, 1985).

Defoe, Daniel, *A Tour through the Whole Island of Great Britain* (2 vols. [first published 1724–6], Everyman edn., London, 1962).

Douglas, Fred, *Gold at Wolf's Crag* (Edinburgh, 1971).

Douglas, William, 'The Exploration of the Historic Cave at Fast Castle', *Scottish Mountaineering Club Journal* xv (1918–20).

_____, 'Fast Castle and Its Owners: Some Notes on their History', *Proceedings of the Society of Antiquaries of Scotland*, lv (1920–1), 56–83.

Duncan, James, *The Descent of the Hepburns of Monkrig* (Edinburgh, 1911).

Edinburgh Archaeological Field Society, *Fast Castle* (Edinburgh, 1977).

Fenton, Alexander, *Scottish Country Life* (Edinburgh, 1976).

Fidler, Kathleen, *The Gold of Fast Castle* (London, 1970).

Fraser, William, *The Douglas Book* (4 vols., Edinburgh, 1885).

Gauld, H. Drummond, *Brave Borderland* (London, 1935).

Graham, Angus, 'Archaeology on a Great Post Road', *Proceedings of the Society of Antiquaries of Scotland*, xcvi (1962–3), 318–47.

Grant, James G., *Edinburgh Register of Testaments* (Edinburgh, 1898).

Harvey, Sir Paul, *The Oxford Companion to English Literature* (Oxford, 1944).

Historical Manuscripts Commission, *Report on the Manuscripts of the Family of Home of Renton* (London, 1876).

_____, *Report on the Manuscripts of the Duke of Athole and the Earl of Home* (London, 1891).

_____, *Report on the Manuscripts of the Earl of Marchmont* (London, 1894).

_____, *Report on the Manuscripts of Colonel David Milne Home* (London, 1902).

_____, *Report on the Manuscripts of Lord Polwarth* (London, 1911).

Home, G. J. N. Logan, *History of the Logan Family* (Edinburgh, 1934).

Inquisitionum Retornatarum Abbreviatio (3 vols., London 1811–16).

International Conference on the History of Cartography, IVth, *The Mapping of Scotland* (Edinburgh, 1971).

Kerr, Robert, *General View of the Agriculture of the County of Berwick* (London, 1809).

Lang, Andrew, *James VI and the Gowrie Mystery* (London, 1902).

Lawson, John P., *Scotland Delineated* (2 vols., London, 1847–54).

Lockhart, John Gibson, *The Life of Sir Walter Scott* (10 vols., Edinburgh, 1902).

Long, A. G., 'Extracts from the Correspondence of James Hardy', *History of the Berwickshire Naturalists' Club*, xxxviii, Part 2 (1969).

MacGibbon, David, and Thomas Ross, *The Castellated and Domestic Architecture of Scotland* (5 vols., Edinburgh, 1887–92).

Maxwell, W. H., *Border Tales and Legends of the Cheviots and Lammermuir* (London, 1852).

Melros Papers, or State Papers and Miscellaneous Correspondence of Thomas, Earl of Melros (Edinburgh, 1837).

Millar, Alexander H., *Fife: Pictorial and Historical* (2 vols., Cupar-Fife, 1895).

Millican, G. B., 'The Division of Coldingham Common, 1763–76', *History of the Berwickshire Naturalists' Club* xlii, Part III (1983), 109–18.

Monniepennie, John, *An Abridgement or Summarie of the Scots Chronicle* (Edinburgh, 1612).

Muirhead, George, *The Birds of Berwickshire* (2 vols., Edinburgh, 1889–95).

Napier, Mark, *Memoirs of John Napier, of Merchiston* (Edinburgh, 1834).

Napier, Robert W., *John Thomson of Duddingston* (Edinburgh, 1919).

New Statistical Account of Scotland: Berwickshire (Edinburgh, 1841).

Paul, Sir James Balfour (ed.), *The Scots Peerage* (9 vols., Edinburgh, 1904–14).

Pelle, M. C., *Landscape Illustrations of the Waverley Novels, by Sir Walter Scott* (n.p., n.d.).

Rankin, Eric, *Cockburnspath* (Edinburgh, 1981).

Register of the Great Seal of Scotland, 1306–1668 (J. B. Paul, J. M. Thomson, and J. H. Stevenson eds.), (11 vols., Edinburgh, 1882–1914).

Register of the Privy Council of Scotland, 1st Ser., 1545–1625 (D. Masson and J. H. Burton eds.), (14 vols., Edinburgh, 1877–98).

_____, 2nd Ser., 1625–60 (P. H. Brown ed.), (8 vols., Edinburgh, 1899–1908).

Richardson, Thomas M., *The Castles of the English and Scottish Borders* (Newcastle upon Tyne, 1834).

Royal Scottish Geographical Society, *The Early Maps of Scotland* (Edinburgh, 1936).

Scott, Sir Walter, *The Bride of Lammermoor* [first published 1819], in the *Waverley Novels*, xiii (Edinburgh, 1830).

_____, *The Provincial Antiquities of Scotland* (2 vols., London, 1826).

Shearer, John, *Old Maps and Map Makers of Scotland* (Stirling, 1905).

Skene, James, *A Series of Sketches of the Existing Localities Alluded to in the Waverley Novels* (Edinburgh, 1829).

Snailham, Richard, *Sangay Survived* (London, 1978).

Stephen, Leslie (ed.), *Dictionary of National Biography* (London, 1885–).

Stirling, Earl of, *Register of Royal Letters* (Edinburgh, 1885).

Taylor, James, *Pictorial History of Scotland* (Edinburgh, 1859).

Thomson, Andrew, *Coldingham Parish and Priory* (Galashiels, 1908).

Thomson, Revd. Thomas (ed.), *Biographical Dictionary of Eminent Scotsmen* (3 vols., London, 1868-70).
Wilson, John McKay and others (eds.), *Tales of the Border* (London, c. 1890).

Typescripts Held or Circulated by the E. A. F. S.

Edinburgh Archaeological Field Society, 'Annual Report, 1985'.
Ashby-Smith, Adrian, '"Jock Trap" Expedition Report' (1976).
Murdoch, K. R. (ed.), 'Newsletter', (1975-).
Ward, J. R., 'Excavations at Fast Castle: The Well' (1987).
_____, and Mitchell, K. L., 'The Barony of Dowlaw: Berwickshire Farming in the Eighteenth Century' (1978).

Index